# Veils in the Vanguard

*Insights of an American Ambassador's Wife in Kuwait*

Catherine Raia Silliman

ISBN-10:1984253972
ISBN-13: 978-1984253972

# DEDICATION

To Doug, Ben, and Zach. We have survived and thrived in the Foreign Service. And to my sister Susan who also understands well life in a foreign culture.

# CONTENTS

Acknowledgments

Preface      1

1   Things Aren't Always as They Appear      3

2   The Long Wait      12

3   Arrival in Kuwait      17

4   Culture Shock      23

5   Gender Segregation and Educated Women      35

6   Leaning Conservative      45

7   Weddings the Kuwaiti Way      60

8   Ramadan Nights      71

9   Imbalance in the Law      80

10   Challenging the Discourse      89

11   Promoting America      99

12   Pearls to Oil      108

13   Lifestyle Chain Reaction      118

14  Catching Up                              132

15  Perils of Wealth                         143

16  The Terror Next Door                     154

17  Education Can Help Bridge the Divide     164

18  Be Careful What You Wish For             172

19  Taking the Reins                         184

Epilogue

# ACKNOWLEDGMENTS

I am most grateful for my husband Doug's support for me to write this book. He was an amazing resource and I will always be in awe of his wisdom. In addition to all the people in Kuwait who shared their lives with me, Stacey Al-Ghawas actually helped me start writing. I still have her magnet on my desk to remind me to "Write. Read. Write. Read." I am grateful to my Arlington, VA, book club whose members also encouraged me to write. My oldest son Ben, a recent William and Mary College graduate at the time, was instrumental in teaching me to research my thoughts and describe them in an engaging and authoritative way. He was especially present in my chapter on Kuwait's natural environment, his area of expertise. My younger son, Zach, gave me insight into life as a young person in Kuwait. I am forever proud that he managed his senior year in a new school with such grace and maturity. Dale Prince, a senior public affairs officer in the Foreign Service, was the first to read my book since he was responsible for clearing it on behalf of the Department of State. I appreciated his grammatical and spelling corrections. He even said he learned a few things! My Mom and Dad, Fil and Ted Raia, have also been very supportive of my writing and publishing this book. My sister Susan, a trilingual expat married to an Italian living in Sweden, is a master editor. She has her own editing and translation company and is very attentive to detail. Growing up, we used to call her Susan Perfect. She was perfect in the way she helped me finish my book.

# PREFACE

I was decidedly ready to accompany my husband by the time he arrived in Kuwait as the U.S. ambassador in August 2014. I saw it as a wonderful opportunity to rekindle my interest in the Middle East and speak Arabic again. I was not prepared, however, to see how much had changed in recent years since prior tours, how little I understood about the Gulf, and why it was so conservative. I felt surprised because I had already lived in Egypt, Syria, Jordan, Pakistan, Tunisia, and Turkey. Why did everything seem so different? I decided to pay attention, listen carefully, read, and experience as much as I could. I took advantage of my connection to the U.S. ambassador, who has enormous access in the country, and I accompanied my husband as often as possible around Kuwait City. I attended his many receptions and dinners at our house. I developed my own contacts and was determined to learn as much as possible. Along the way, I made wonderful friends who gave me great joy and amazing memories I will cherish always.

In this book, I try to share my experience as the wife of the U.S. ambassador in Kuwait between 2014 and 2016. By unwrapping the country piece by piece, I hope to provide a small window into Islam and Arab culture during this tense period when Islamic State of Iraq and Syria (ISIS) had managed to establish its bloody and destructive caliphate so close to Kuwait's tiny border. Additionally, I hope my book will spotlight the 25 years that have passed since the United States and an international coalition of forces liberated Kuwait from Saddam Hussein's occupation in 1991. I, like probably most Americans, saw the Gulf War, codenamed Operation Desert Shield, through western media, following closely our own troops fighting their first ground war in decades. Learning the Kuwaiti side of the Iraqi invasion was particularly poignant for me. Their painful memories affect Kuwait to this day and weigh heavily on its future decisions.

This account of 21st century Kuwait from my vantage point as a diplomatic spouse also provides a glimpse into U.S. Foreign Service life and raising an American family in the Middle East and South Asia. While it has not always been easy, it has been a privilege and honor to serve as representatives of the United States abroad over the past three decades.

# CHAPTER ONE

## *Things Aren't Always As They Appear*

When I was a junior year abroad student at the American University in Cairo (AUC) in 1979, the Arab women I knew wore miniskirts and tight jeans. My Palestinian roommate, who grew up in Saudi Arabia, used to wear jeans so tight she had to lie on her bed each morning just to tug them up and close them. She rolled back and forth, looking so uncomfortable I couldn't help but wonder if it was worth it. She slept with curlers each night to ensure perfect hair in the morning. In Cairo, I felt plain and a little intimidated by my Egyptian and Arab dorm mates who were always so carefully groomed and beautifully dressed in the latest European fashion. AUC was an elite private school and these women were from mostly wealthy families. Their wealth was in stark contrast to the streets outside, where jagged potholes and disorganized traffic posed a constant challenge. While our glamorously dressed roommates in their high-heeled shoes were shuttled to school each morning by their private drivers, my American friends and I were more practical, walking or taking taxis to class and wearing t-shirts and jeans. We reserved makeup and nice clothes for evenings out and even then, we were a lot more casual than our bejeweled counterparts.

Looking back, I should not have mistaken their glamour for wanting the same progressive lifestyle I had in the States. These women were still living their lives according to the expectations of their parents and society. They could be educated and have jobs, but it was never guaranteed that they would live in a society that would provide them the same opportunities or even encourage them to have the same independence that women have in the United States. Their culture was more a part of their lives than I had realized, thoughts and traditions that were quite capable of withstanding the ephemeral trends of fashion and the intrusion of western and liberal ideas.

When I graduated from college in 1981, there was no question about whether I would work. The economy was good and jobs were plentiful in the Reagan era for college graduates. I quickly found my first job in Washington, D.C. and moved into a townhouse with four other young female graduates. We called ourselves the "young professionals," or "YP's." It was very exciting for all of us to be in the workforce as we believed we were breaking through barriers just by our presence in offices and businesses across the city. The opportunities we had when we graduated from our universities in the States were not the same for our Arab and Egyptian counterparts we left behind at AUC. In fact, I am sure our Arab and Egyptian roommates found a much different set of circumstances when they graduated from AUC.

This college year abroad was not my initiation to the Middle East. The first time I visited a Muslim country was in the summer of 1976 when I was a 16-year-old American Field Service (AFS) exchange student in Izmir, Turkey. I was completely new to the Middle East, and was curious about its religion of Islam. Listening to Muslims pray five times a day was spellbinding and I was enchanted to learn that they were called to prayer from atop the tall minaret towers connected to these architecturally pleasing buildings called mosques. I was charmed by this whole new world, energized by the intoxicating blend of East and West, which later I understood to be uniquely found in Turkey, known as the "bridge" between the Asian and European worlds. In between the five calls to prayer each day, I remember hearing ABBA's latest hits blasting through public speakers in the main square of the small Aegean farm town not far from Izmir where I lived that summer.

The young Turkish women I met planned to go to college and they dressed pretty much the way I did, though they did not wear shorts, nor were they seen in public without their best clothes and plenty of maquillage. I was there to help them learn English. In my Turkish AFS family, only the widowed mother wore a headscarf. She prayed five times a day and when she did, it seemed like a signal for her youngest son to climb playfully on her back. The rest of us gently walked around her in the small apartment we shared, going about our business. Praying seemed like something older people did.

When I went to Tufts University in 1977, I wanted to make a career of seeing the world and so I chose to study International Relations. While at Tufts, I sifted through the library's collection of overseas colleges and programs to choose where I might study during my junior year abroad, and I selected the American University in Cairo (AUC) because I wanted to learn more about Islam and the Middle East. As a junior year abroad student at AUC from 1979 to 1980, I had the opportunity to study with some excellent visiting American Middle East scholars. Among them was Professor Malcolm Kerr from the University of California in Los Angeles who later served as the President of the American University in Beirut in 1982. Lebanese Hezbollah tragically gunned him down outside his office in 1984.

While I was in Cairo, a group of radical Iranian students stormed the U.S. embassy in Tehran on November 4, 1979 and took more than 60 American hostages. It is possible that everything changed at that moment in the Middle East without our realizing. Overnight, Egyptian soldiers dressed in black with helmets on and bayonets at their side surrounded AUC, a landmark institution associated with the United States located then just off Cairo's Tahrir Square. Although as American students in Egypt we felt very far from the crisis in Tehran with its newly installed radical theocracy, the Egyptian government was not taking any chances and moved to protect U.S. interests the best it could. As students, we did not focus on the possibility that this revolution marked the beginning of the rise in Islamic fundamentalism, or worse, radicalism and terrorism, across the region. Instead, we carried on as usual and even made plans to see as much of the Middle East as we could during our winter break.

In January 1980, I travelled with a small group of American students to Lebanon, Syria, Jordan, and Israel. It was an incredible trip that sadly could not be duplicated today, given the war in Syria and its fallout in Lebanon. On our return to Cairo from Israel, we crossed the Sinai Peninsula to take advantage of the Egypt-Israel Peace Treaty signed less than a year before in March 1979. We were among the first tourists to do this. It was a shock that little more than a year after I had left Egypt, Islamic fundamentalist army officers assassinated one of the treaty's signatories, President Anwar Sadat, on October 6, 1981. The world had hoped this treaty would mark the beginning of peace in the region, but regrettably the situation today has instead descended into anger, disillusionment and instability.

After graduating from Tufts, I was still passionate about the Middle East, despite the growing dangers in the region. I was hired as a reporter for the Saudi Research and Marketing Company in its Washington, D.C. bureau. I'm pretty sure I got the job in a phone interview because I knew where the Shatt al-Arab was located; this is the waterway formed by the confluence of the Euphrates and Tigris Rivers in southern Iraq. I wrote stories for their international newspaper *Asharq al-Awsat* (translated "Middle East") published in London and the local English language newspaper *Arab News* published in Jeddah, Saudi Arabia. I worked in their Washington bureau for a year and even had my own pass to attend briefings at the White House. It was 1981 and many Arab journalists were angry that the Israelis had bombed Iraq's Osirak nuclear plant. Looking back, it would have been a disaster if Saddam Hussein had had access to nuclear weapons when he invaded Kuwait less than a decade later in 1990.

Meanwhile, the Saudi brothers who owned the Arab publications I worked for were consumed in an internal family struggle and after I returned from a summer vacation in 1982, a decision was made to close the D.C. office. I had applied to graduate programs after my college graduation the previous year and thus I decided to go back to school. So off I went to the University of Chicago to pursue a Master of Arts Degree in Middle Eastern Studies. There, I studied Arabic and was required to take Chicago's prestigious Islamic Civilization courses based on Marshall G. S. Hodgson's three-volume series *"The Venture of Islam; Conscience and History in a World Civilization"*. It is only now that I can appreciate what a unique experience I had. Hodgson is remembered for his distinctive efforts to incorporate the study of Islam as part of world history. We learned about Islam in the context of the ancient and medieval civilizations that dominated the region it eventually ruled.[i] At Chicago, I learned to appreciate the Middle East as a tapestry of ancient civilizations, fallen empires, religious diversity, and modern politics. For me it was an exciting place to learn about the world. Like Hodgson, who died in 1968, I had no idea that this incredibly rich region would decline today into so much chaos.

While at the University of Chicago, I applied to the State Department and worked there upon graduation from 1984 to 1998. During that time, I met my husband Doug, a Foreign Service Officer, through mutual friends in Washington. We had both served overseas while single, he in Tunis and I in Amman, including a summer in Damascus, in the late eighties. We were married in June 1990 and looked forward to working and living together overseas.

Not long after we were married, Saddam Hussein's Iraqi forces invaded Kuwait. This was our first exposure to Kuwait. October that same year, my dad, who was serving as the

Deputy Commander of the Cutler Army Hospital at Fort Devens Army Base in Ayer, MA, received orders to head out to Saudi Arabia as commander of the 46th Combat Support Hospital to serve in Operation Desert Shield and prevent the Saddam Hussein's forces from entering into Saudi Arabia. I never expected my dad to care for the wounded in a war in the Middle East. Congress heavily debated whether our troops should go to war in 1990, as our country had not been in a war since Vietnam. In the end, President George H. W. Bush made the right decision to act and free Kuwait.

Then came our first assignment as a married couple. It was Islamabad, Pakistan from 1993 – 1996 where we took our first son at just three months old. Shortly after this tour I decided to resign from government service. It had been a rough time. Terrorism was on the rise, culminating in the deadly Al-Qaeda bombing at the Egyptian embassy in Islamabad on November 19, 1995. The Egyptian embassy was just down the street from our embassy. Our son Ben, two years old at the time, was at home with his visiting grandparents. I had gone to the window in my office at the embassy to see what was going on and could feel the large second blast that occurred not long after the first breaching charge. I was lucky. Now, embassy personnel are trained never to go to the window when there is an explosion. Instead we are required to duck and cover. Needless to say, the experience was more than I had bargained for. So, it was then in my late thirties that I left the State Department and turned to raising a family - though this did not mean that I would stop learning or stop working. But my husband Doug had the ambition and he was set to go full throttle with his Foreign Service career. In the coming years, we went on to assignments in Tunisia, Jordan, and Turkey.

So, I had been living in and out of the region in Muslim-majority countries for almost 40 years by the time I arrived in Kuwait in 2014. Upon my entry into the country, more than three decades after my college year experience in Cairo, I felt as though my life had come full circle. I was immediately intrigued by the women I found in Kuwait and could not help but reflect back to 1979 in the Arab women's hostel in Cairo. These were not the same women I had left at AUC so many years ago. I could not have imagined my Egyptian friends then considering for a moment covering their meticulously groomed appearances. But in Kuwait 35 years later, the local women were everywhere I looked in society, and yet there were so many unexpected traditional trappings such as gender segregation and covering. Still the women were vibrant and social, and I found them very approachable, open, and friendly as I had in other countries I had lived in the region.

I soon learned that, in Kuwait, 46 percent of women worked, below the U.S. rate of 57 percent[ii], but almost double the rate of women in the labor force across the Middle East and North Africa region.[iii] And with that, I assumed Kuwaiti women would also be much more progressive than those in other countries. But I quickly realized that things were not as they appeared. Although Kuwaiti women were fairly well represented in the workplace, very few had advanced to the corporate boardroom or been promoted into the highest levels of government. One reason, I learned, was that by the age of 50, most women had decided to retire due to generous retirement packages. Thus, women were not staying long enough in their careers to make it into the senior ranks. Many were also not pursuing postgraduate degrees to give them the necessary skills. While 55 percent of working women hold a bachelor's degree, only 14 percent hold advanced degrees.[iv] I began to wonder whether Kuwaiti women really wanted more since they already seemed to have an awful lot. They had education, careers, and financial independence, and they had time to raise their families. What seemed to be missing in my mind was the expressed feminist will to achieve equal rights with men, especially in a system stacked against women because of its patriarchal roots.

As I found in Egypt so many years ago, Kuwaiti culture has also been resilient to the press of western influence and progressive ideas. Nowhere was this more apparent than when observing Kuwaiti women in the luxurious shopping malls in the city. Although I saw plenty of women purchasing western clothing in the high-end fashion stores, I was not seeing many of them wearing their outfits, at least not in public. This was because so many women chose to wear their western clothing under their *abayyas*, the long black oversized cloak draping over their shoulders down to the floor. Many also were electing to wear a long black veil, known as the *hijab* in Arabic, sometimes worn in different styles and colors, to hide their hair. Some were even wearing the *niqab*, a black cloth that hides their faces, leaving only their eyes exposed. The wife of the Australian ambassador noted one evening that, even though Kuwaiti women were in long black *abayyas* and *hijabs*, they were still beautiful. They certainly cared about their appearance. Their kohl-lined eyes and thick black eyelashes, a custom originating in the desert to protect against the sun, affirmed their beauty. Designer sunglasses, handbags, and shoes provided a small glimpse into their individual sense of style, but not necessarily into their educational backgrounds, their careers, their personal goals, or the expectations they had for their children.

A "*muhajiba*" (a woman who wears the *hijab*) explained to me that wearing her veil was like wearing a shirt. "You would not go out of the house without a shirt much as you would not leave without wearing a *hijab*.'" She also happened to be an engineer who was very serious about her career and raising her family at the same time. The number of women wearing the *hijab* has increased significantly in the past few decades. Ironically, this is happening even as more women are joining the workforce and participating in public life more than ever before.

The contradiction of women choosing to be professionals and living active lives while at the same time dressing according to their tribal traditions is perplexing to western observers, especially to those who do not understand the culture. But even for some older Kuwaitis, it is mystifying as to why western fashion, which was the norm in the 1960's, 70's, and

80's, has given way to the veil. This older generation, many of whom still wear their western clothes in public, understands the culture, but they do not agree that it should dictate the way they dress. What made Kuwait compelling to me was that there was a steady discourse between liberal Kuwaitis who aspire toward western ways and conservatives who seek to stay within the confines of their traditional culture.

So, upon my arrival in Kuwait in September 2014 as the wife of the U.S. ambassador, I could not help but dive into the Middle East again, and I found that my position opened many doors for me to access a clearly changed Middle East. I had a keen interest and I was in a unique position. What was this Kuwaiti culture well into the 21st century? I immediately felt an urgency to record my insights while I explored this area. I decided to write this book, an ambitious project, but one I felt obliged to do as a way of helping to narrow the huge void in our cultural understanding, to share with others the complexities of this region and in particular, shed light on the important role that women play.

# CHAPTER TWO

## *The Long Wait*

The years just prior to our arrival in Kuwait were a critical time. I remained at our previous post in Ankara, Turkey, as Doug was the Deputy Chief of Mission at the U.S. embassy in Baghdad, Iraq, and family were not permitted to accompany Baghdad staff. In April 2013 Doug received a call that he was being considered to be then-President Obama's next U.S. Ambassador to Kuwait. This was great news for us. Having started in the summer 2011 as the Political Counselor, Doug was on his second year in Baghdad. The U.S. embassy in the Green Zone was still taking rocket fire from pro-Iranian forces in Iraq. Iraq's Prime Minister Nouri al-Maliki at the time was also succumbing to heavy pressure from Iran and failing to secure from his government the necessary immunity from prosecution for U.S. troops to stay on the ground. Thus, the last U.S. troops assigned to Iraq departed by the end of 2011 in accordance with the agreement signed under former President George W. Bush. The U.S. leadership at the time did not want to leave its troops in Iraq, in harm's way, without the necessary immunities.

The U.S. embassy in Baghdad, meanwhile, was left to its own resources to protect and support itself.[vi] It had to find new supply lines to care and feed itself without the help of the elaborate U.S. military logistics operations. By the time Doug stepped up to be the number two at the embassy in summer 2012, he inherited the job of shrinking the U.S. embassy footprint in Baghdad. His job quickly became about reducing the cost of the mission and cutting thousands of positions. When he left in summer 2013, the embassy had managed to cut itself by more than half.[vii]

Needless to say, we were thrilled to have Doug be considered for the next U.S. Ambassador to Kuwait. It was certainly a sign that his hard work was being recognized. He had always wanted to achieve the rank of Ambassador and he had hoped serving in a tough assignment like Baghdad would help his chances. Now I was back in Arlington, Virginia, having returned the previous summer from Ankara, Turkey, after four years, and I was hesitant about settling in too much because I knew there was a chance we would move overseas after Doug's tour in Iraq. I was also happy to hear the news. I figured we would be in Kuwait sometime in fall 2013. I had no idea that it would take another full year before the U.S. Senate would confirm Doug and we would arrive in Kuwait.

I was relieved to have Doug at home in Virginia when his Iraq tour ended in September 2013; after all, we had had separate households for two years. But now the start date for this next assignment was unclear because of the necessary Senate confirmation. Waiting is not easy when one is accustomed to the daily adrenalin fix of managing the U.S. embassy in Baghdad; Doug really enjoyed the work and the responsibility he had in Baghdad. I also worried about our younger son. He was going to enter his junior year in high school. We had initially told him he might start his junior year in Kuwait. That scenario quickly became less likely. Somehow, he shielded himself from his parents' angst and went on to enjoy his junior year in northern Virginia. My older son Ben was at the College of William and Mary at the time and so he was not affected by all the uncertainty.

During the wait, we had occasional duties in preparation for the ambassadorial appointment. There was a photo opportunity with Secretary of State John Kerry, and we attended the Ambassadorial Seminar where we met other nominees who were waiting in the nomination queue and their spouses. This was when I began to hear rather anxious stories from the other nominees. "My wife quit her job months ago and she is ready to kill me." "I sold my house. Now I have to find a place to rent without knowing for how long." These comments made me realize we were not alone in our desire to know exactly when we would be able to leave. Everyone had reason to hope that the process would go quickly.

The White House meanwhile announced that Doug was formally nominated as the next U.S. Ambassador to Kuwait on December 13, 2013. Once his name left the White House, we became part of the Congressional confirmation process. Executive branch appointments for senior public positions require approval by the legislative branch. That year, however, the Senate acted slowly on President Obama's ambassadorial nominations. The bottleneck in the confirmation process slowed further when then-Senate Majority Leader Harry Reid, Democrat of Nevada, invoked the "nuclear option" in November 2013. By eliminating filibusters for most nominations by the President, the hope was that this would speed things up in the Congress. Instead, the Republicans found legal loopholes that slowed down the process even more. Doug's nomination was sent back from the Congress to the White House on January 6, 2014. All the nominees would have to prepare a whole new set of papers to be nominated again in the new year.

Doug submitted his new set of papers to the White House and was re-nominated in late January 2014. Time passed. Then we received notification that the Senate Foreign Relations Committee would hold his hearing on February 13, 2014. There was lots of excitement and Doug carefully prepared his testimony. As luck would have it, there was a paralyzing snowstorm that day. The government decided to shut down. Virginia's Democratic Senator Tim Kaine, the sub-committee chairman, managed to get to Capitol Hill along with one other Senator on his committee, Republican Senator John Barrasso from Wyoming. Once we heard there would be enough members to hold the hearing, we drove to the Ballston subway station and took the Metro to DC's Union Station. We found a cleared sidewalk to a very quiet Dirksen Building on the Senate side of the Capitol Building. The only thing missing that day was media coverage due to the bad weather. There was not even a stenographer to record the oral questions and answers. The hearing was, however, a very warm and cozy experience shared with three other nominees and their families.

They were Joseph Westphal to be Ambassador of Saudi Arabia, Matthew Tueller to be Ambassador to the Republic of Yemen, and Mark Gilbert to be Ambassador to New Zealand. We had gotten to know Joe and his wife Linda in Washington. Matt was the former Ambassador to Kuwait and we had met his wife DeNeece at the Ambassadors' Seminar held at the State Department earlier in the spring. As a political appointee, Mark Gilbert and his family were truly moved to be a part of this grand tradition of the congressional hearing during which the nominees read a prepared statement followed by a question and answer session. Needless to say, it was a proud moment for all.

Now past the Senate Foreign Relations Committee, the nominees had to be approved by the full Congress. So, began another long wait. By early July 2014, numbers of ambassadorial and senior State Department nominations were stacking up in the Senate. It started looking like we may not even make it to Kuwait by fall 2014 for our son to start his senior year. Doug worked on the United States–Africa Leaders' Summit held in Washington that summer, worthy work which kept him sharp through the difficult wait. Congress finally confirmed him on July 10, 2014. Doug was very fortunate, as many nominees would not be confirmed until several months later.

I witnessed Doug's swearing-in ceremony on August 11, held in the Franklin Room on the State Department's prestigious seventh floor, a packed room which broke out in a warm and loud cheer. We as his family were moved to see Doug had earned the support of his colleagues through his thirty years of service. He arrived in Kuwait to take up his official post at U.S. Embassy Kuwait on August 21, 2014, accompanied by our son Zach who had meanwhile managed to enroll in the American School of Kuwait for his senior year.

# CHAPTER THREE

## *Arrival in Kuwait*

I arrived in Kuwait City on September 14, 2014. My husband and son happily met me at Kuwait's International Airport. We were immediately whisked off to the large ornate VIP reception hall with golden chandeliers. Seated on decorative couches placed against the walls in proper *diwaniyya* style, were other Gulf dignitaries. They all were wearing their long white robes called *dishdashas* and head coverings called *keffiyehs*, also known as *gutras*. Welcome to Kuwait, I thought. There was not a woman in sight.

As we waited for my bags, I was offered my first Arabic coffee in the Gulf, followed by tea and water. I think everyone who comes to the Arab world is immediately taken by the hospitality. We then walked through the airport escorted by my husband's large entourage of Kuwaiti security men, well-armed and clad in tan fatigues. My first reaction was not about feeling important, but instead feeling a certain amount of fear. I kept thinking about what it was that we were being protected from and I imagined all sorts of hidden threats. I looked over at my son Zach who was smiling, happy to see me, and already used to the scene. We smiled and laughed despite everything going on around us.

I would later grow accustomed to being surrounded and followed by a security detail whenever I was with Doug. Sometimes we thought we had lost them because we tend to walk fast but they would always quickly reappear. The rule was that Doug was required to have a security detail whenever he was outside our embassy compound. This included our mundane trips to the grocery store, to weekly Mass, and our walks along the sea on the corniche. Our passion is biking but we were unable to convince the guards to cycle with us. They just did not feel they could protect us, but I suppose I could not really see any of them actually wanting to bike with us. We are beholden to our security guards, and so we adopted and did what they felt comfortable doing. I eventually found my own intrepid group, and without my husband, we would go off the compound on Friday mornings, the first day of the local weekend, early enough to miss the dangerous traffic that would occur once people arrived for Friday prayers at the local mosques.

Leaving the airport on our way to our new home on the U.S. embassy compound, we drove through the city and along the coast. Kuwait reminded me of the west coast of Florida where my parents live, and I could see some similarities. There were wide boulevards lined with palm trees and the blue-green sea could be seen from the road along a well-groomed corniche. The key difference, aside from being immersed in eastern culture, was that the temperature outside was much hotter than anything I had ever experienced. It was almost 120 degrees! It felt like I had walked into the blast of heat you feel opening the oven door to check your baking.

The official residence in Kuwait, known as the Chief of Mission Residence or "CMR", is considered among the most ornate of the newer ambassadors' residences that have been built on U.S. embassy compounds. More and more ambassadors' residences are being built on embassy compounds to provide greater security. U.S. Marine security guards, who have historically protected U.S. embassies abroad, provide additional protection to us when they are located on the compound. I do miss the normalcy of being in a regular neighborhood as opposed to living inside the fortress that is our U.S. embassy. But I suppose once you reach the level of U.S. ambassador, living a normal life in a neighborhood is something that is not going to happen. A fellow ambassador's wife reminded me that if your residence was located outside the embassy compound, security personnel would have to patrol the grounds around your house constantly, and this could be even more invasive to your private life. I grew to accept my well-fortified new home on the compound conveniently located near the main Chancery, a minute walk to work for my husband.

The ambassador's residence in Kuwait was built in the 1990's after the liberation of Kuwait. The Kuwaiti government, in a gesture of thanks for the role played by the United States, provided a large tract of land next to the Amir's striking Bayan Palace. The thought was that this location would provide added security since the area was already well protected for the country's ruler. The Kuwaiti government also provided $100 million to the State Department to build a new U.S. embassy.[viii] With this infusion of funds, the CMR was built with the finest materials including inlaid Italian marble floors and walls adorned with fine oriental woodcarvings. The home is truly beautiful. While the nineties were a time of building and rebirth in Kuwait, the U.S. government budget crunch, however, caused the State Department to limit the size of the residence. As a result, the U.S. ambassador's home is quite small to entertain large groups of people. For instance, the only way we could possibly entertain 86 members of the Kuwait Chapter of the *Chaine de Rotisseurs* for dinner was for the organization to pay for and set up a large tent outside in our garden.

The very next day after my arrival in Kuwait, September 15, 2014, I learned I was invited to attend the ceremony in which Doug would finally present his credentials to the head of the Kuwaiti government, Amir Sheikh Sabah Al-Ahmad al-

Jaber al-Sabah. The Amir had just returned to Kuwait from his summer holiday and an official ceremony was quickly arranged for all the new ambassadors to present their credentials. For Doug, this meant presenting two letters signed by the President of the United States. The first was a "letter of recall" to withdraw the credentials of the former U.S. ambassador. The second was a "letter of credence" that designated the new U.S. ambassador. The head of the host country government must receive and officially acknowledge these letters before an ambassadorship becomes official.

It is tradition here for a senior Kuwaiti protocol officer to escort a new ambassador to the credential ceremony held at the exquisite Bayan Palace transported in a Bentley automobile. How exciting I thought! When I saw the beautiful car roll up alongside the residence, I thought I would hop in next to my husband. It was here I learned I was not going to travel with my ambassador husband to the Palace. That was the preserve of the Kuwaiti Protocol officer. Instead, I would travel separately in an embassy vehicle with senior embassy staff.

I was a little surprised, quite honestly. I still remember sipping champagne at the ambassador's residence in Islamabad, Pakistan, following the credential ceremony for our new U.S. ambassador there. Both my husband and I were working at the U.S. embassy in Islamabad on January 26, 1996, when Ambassador Tom Simons presented his credentials. I recall both he and his wife talking about their ride together in a horse-drawn carriage down Islamabad's Constitution Avenue as part of the tradition for newly accredited ambassadors. I remember Mrs. Simons even wore a fancy hat that day! Somehow I had imagined my experience would be similarly grand.

I was not disappointed though. Once we arrived at the Bayan Palace, we met several other ambassadors and their spouses waiting to present credentials. Among them were British Ambassador Matthew Lodge and his wife Alexia. We waited together in a small but very beautiful *diwaniyya*, the Kuwaiti equivalent of a salon where couches and chairs line the walls leaving the center of the room open. After a couple of hours of chatting and getting to know each other while waiting for the Amir, we were called to follow the Kuwaiti protocol staff to a magnificent ceremonial hall.

The Bayan Palace had only been recently renovated. I could not help but notice with awe how the walls sparkled white with elegant touches of gold. This was not your typical Louis XIVth affectation sometimes seen in the Middle East. It was something much more tasteful and sophisticated. Clearly the interior designers of this Palace knew what they were doing when they created the sensation of a Palace of an oil-rich state with enough simplicity not to overwhelm. The Bayan Palace originally opened in 1986. It sits on more than 346 acres and houses meeting rooms, offices, a state-of-the-art theater, and a botanical garden in addition to the sumptuous ceremonial hall.

During the ceremony, I was instructed to sit along the side of the grand hall next to our embassy's Deputy Chief of Mission, Joey Hood, and Office of Defense Cooperation Commander, Major General Scott Williams. Our chairs were upholstered in bright yellow satin giving the room a delightful energy. They showed nicely against the magnificent pastel floral carpet that covered the floor with thick and comfortable pile. Doug and the nine other ambassadors remained in a holding room, each waiting for his or her turn to meet with the Amir. Doug was finally called to present his credentials and sat in the empty chair next to the Amir. I looked on as they sat together, exchanging greetings and salutations. The Amir was interested in Turkish politics that day and inquired about Doug's view of Recip Tayyip Erdogan who had just maneuvered himself to be Turkey's newly elected president after years as the prime minister. With extensive experience working on Turkey, including three years as deputy chief of mission at the U.S. embassy in Ankara, Doug proved he could give good counsel and deliver it in Arabic no less. I was very proud that Doug was now ambassador after 30 years in the Foreign Service.

I was then summoned to approach the Amir, and he warmly shook my hand as did all the Kuwaiti ministers and protocol officers in attendance. Kuwaiti men are really very open and welcoming. They quite often welcomed me with a kiss on both cheeks when I went to social events in the evening. I was happy to see that there was not the slightest hesitation about shaking my hand. Of course, handshaking is only an issue if there are conservatives in the room who prefer not to acknowledge women in public. This was clearly not the case on that day, as the ruling family is generally progressive, something I would ascertain later as I was able to meet many of the Al-Sabah family during my stay in Kuwait. But whether I should attend an event or not, shake hands with men or not, decide whether to wear long skirts and cover my shoulders or not, would all have to be considered now that I was the wife of the U.S. ambassador. These questions suddenly loomed large, since what I chose to do now might actually be noticed.

# CHAPTER FOUR

## *Culture Shock*

Thus, I began my quest to define my role as the wife of the new American ambassador in Kuwait. I arrived with the idea that I wanted to be an active spouse, part of a visible team. The State Department had got me thinking about this during the Ambassadorial Seminar I attended before my departure. I became especially encouraged when the Department asked my husband to prepare a short video as part of his introduction to Kuwait and welcomed me as part of the buzz. Doug very much wanted me in it and I was happy to participate. The experience convinced me that I wanted our experience in Kuwait to be one that we would share together. He chose to film at George Washington University, where he received a Master of Arts degree, but also where the State of Kuwait has bestowed a significant endowment and has a deep connection. It was exciting to see our video picked up on Kuwait's social media and TV stations. I felt sure we were going to be a dynamic duo during our inaugural ambassadorial tour.

Once in Kuwait, though, I was thrown by the fact that Kuwaiti wives do not generally appear in public with their husbands. They tend not to participate in public events, nor do they typically accompany their husbands to receptions or dinner parties. As female family members, their domain was generally separate from men, behind a curtain -- a veil -- in Arabic known as the *hijab*. If they choose to go out, it is more likely to be to places with other women and they would probably cover until they are sure no men are present.

There are, however, many Kuwaiti women in the public eye, including female politicians, TV personalities, and heads of nonprofit organizations, bankers, doctors, lawyers, engineers, political activists, and art dealers, among many other professionals. Many cover; some do not. The issue is not whether it is appropriate for Kuwaiti women to participate in public events as professionals. My focus was whether there was a public role for a *wife* of a foreign official in an environment where wives generally do not participate. In discussing the issue at the gym one day, a British woman said she felt there was no need whatsoever for the British public to know anything about or see the spouses of elected and public officials. She simply had no interest. In Britain, after all, there was already enough preoccupation with the spouses of the royal family. An American woman in the same conversation felt differently. She wanted to see and learn about the spouses of public officials; it could provide important insight into the character of the official. Her attitude of course reflected America's tradition of wanting to know about presidential spouses and see them involved in public life.

This conversation was not necessarily addressing my particular situation, but it gave me some different perspectives on the role of spouses of public officials in different countries. What I needed was to learn how Kuwaitis would view me accompanying my husband in public because this was what I ultimately wanted to do. Subliminally, I wanted to share my culture in which husbands and wives are seen together. Certainly, this is what I had envisioned, but now I was faced with things being different in Kuwait.

I thought back on the State Department course to help spouses of ambassadors prepare for their role before they arrive at post. While we learned very useful things like drafting speeches and how to deal with an aggressive press, we did not talk about what spouses of American ambassadors should do in a patriarchal society where female family members are not generally seen in public. My very experienced predecessor, DeNeece Tueller, had served in Kuwait twice before her husband, Matt, became the previous U.S. ambassador to Kuwait. She was also in the Ambassadorial Seminar with me since her husband was moving on to be the next U.S. Ambassador to Yemen. She had described Kuwait as amazing and had forewarned me that I would have a very heavy social schedule. I could be out every night of the week if I wanted.

DeNeece had regaled me with stories of Kuwaiti wedding parties she had attended in which only women participated and how much fun they were. The women, she said, were so at ease and comfortable dancing and expressing themselves, free from the watchful eyes of men. The parties sounded as though they were the ultimate expression of feminism. It all sounded very exciting and something I had never experienced before. In the brief time we had together, I did not think to ask her about whether I would be welcome where Kuwaiti female family members were not participating. Was it okay to attend a dinner of a Kuwaiti host without his wife present? Could I accompany my husband to public events when no other Kuwaiti wives would attend? These questions occurred to me only after I had arrived. After all, these issues are not problematic in our culture in the States.

Since I had never lived in the Gulf before, it was going to take time for me to feel comfortable. One thing was clear: on Kuwait's diplomatic circuit where the diplomatic community rotates through a hectic schedule of national day receptions and dinner parties, I was not meeting many Kuwaitis, especially Kuwaiti women. The women I did meet initially were either foreigners married to Kuwaitis or wives of other ambassadors. The International Women's Group (IWG), in which wives of ambassadors were honorary members, was another venue where I mostly met foreign females. Between IWG events and the diplomatic circuit representing 133 countries,[ix] it was possible to spend almost all of my time with non-Kuwaitis if I wanted. How was I going to learn about the culture if I was not meeting Kuwaitis? How would I be able to determine my role if I was not talking to Kuwaiti women directly? I was frustrated because even when I met important Kuwaitis, I was not meeting their wives.

One Saturday afternoon soon after I had arrived, we were invited with our son to the beach house of a senior Kuwaiti official. Upon arriving at his stylish chalet, our Kuwaiti host immediately apologized that his wife could not attend. That was fine. Spouses should not be expected to drop everything to entertain their husband's foreign guests, but then I discovered I would literally be the only woman at the beach house that day. Only the official's sons, not even his daughters, were present. His European male house manager and male chef were in the kitchen preparing the delicious lunch. It just felt strange being there without any other woman. I respected the Kuwaiti official very much for including me that day, but the experience made me more anxious about my role.

My hesitancy peaked a month later at our National Day celebration. We held it in December just after Thanksgiving in 2014 because the weather is much cooler. Our true National Day, Independence Day celebrated on July 4, is just too hot to celebrate outdoors when temperatures can reach over 110 degrees. All embassies host their country's national day. Most hold their event at a hotel. We hold our event outside in our embassy garden and invite some 2,000 guests. Of course, they don't all attend, but it is our way to show our appreciation to all our friends and supporters in Kuwait. Having never done this before as the ambassador's spouse, I was not sure what was expected of me. Was I to be on stage with the senior Kuwaiti guest who would of course arrive without his wife? Should I help cut the ceremonial cake after speeches by the ambassador and our senior Kuwaiti guest?

I decided I should be on the stage. But then a local Arab photographer covering the event derailed my confidence.

As we were waiting for the arrival of our official Kuwaiti government guest, the photographer suggested that I not be in the pictures so he could get a better photo of the ambassador and the senior Kuwaiti official when he arrived. That was it! I fled into the crowd and hid. Yes, I was overly sensitive, but I was not going to put myself out there without knowing for sure I was welcome. Silly, I know, but I had received so many mixed messages about the role of female family members in Kuwaiti society that I just wasn't ready.

After that I needed to resolve my role and fast. This was not the way I wanted to experience Kuwait. So, I decided to read more about women in the Gulf, especially those from tribal backgrounds. Why did wives not appear in public? If I could understand more about the society, I was sure I would feel more comfortable.

According to Margaret K. Nydell, author of "Understanding Arabs," the main reason for gender separation in the Arab world, especially on the Arabian Peninsula, has been the overarching importance of maintaining family honor. Even the appearance of something potentially damaging to the family should be avoided at all costs. In the desert, loss of family honor could have serious repercussions. An entire family or tribe could be cut off from food and water. Or they could be subjected to relentless raids and blood feuds. More socially significant, their daughters would jeopardize any hope of receiving worthy wedding proposals.

In the Arab world, women are the ones, it seems, who have had to bear the responsibility for protecting family honor. It has somehow become understood and accepted that men cannot be expected to control themselves around the beauty and sexual attraction of women, and so women are responsible for not bringing attention onto themselves. This is the accepted natural order of the sexes in this part of the world. If a woman reveals her beauty, then she is inviting a man's attention and he cannot be held responsible for his natural, even violent, urges toward her. The problem is not so much about what a woman does as much as about what it may *look*

27

like she is doing in terms of attracting the opposite sex. With so much potential for misinterpretation, women have gladly used the cover of the veil to avoid all possible appearances that might impugn them and their family's honor. For this reason, also, many women prefer gender-separated environments to avoid any possible innuendo.

As a mother of two sons, I am saddened that boys in conservative Arabian families are held to a standard that does not require self-control when it comes to the opposite sex. It is almost a form of discrimination that more is not expected of young males. During the *Eid* holidays, for example, I saw a sign in front of a government-run beach club that read, "No *Shabbab* (Young Men). Entrance for Families Only. It is Forbidden for Young Men to Enter During the Holidays." Wow, I thought, my own sons would not be able to go to this beach on their own. The concern, of course, was that young single men could not be trusted to refrain from being a bother to the girls on the beach.

Gender segregation appears to be getting stricter in Kuwait. In 2016, for example, a new Ministry of Interior law mandated that the local cinema franchise, Cinescape, had to strictly enforce separate seating sections for families and bachelors. In an Instagram ad, Cinescape made it known that it would require purchasers of tickets to agree that any booking or purchase made in the wrong seating section would be in violation of Cinescape seating rules. Therefore, customers could lose their chance to attend the movie or have their tickets refunded. [x] Again, I thought of my own sons. They would have to be cautioned about this rule if they were to decide to go the movies without us, their family, because it was perceived that they could not be trusted to sit near girls.

According to the State Department's Human Rights Report in 2014, single young men are prevented from purchasing apartments on their own in urban areas and the U.S. government has classified this as a violation of human rights. Young men are being denied the right to establish themselves independently to pursue their livelihoods without being married. The underlying reason is that Arab society has decided men cannot be trusted to live alone in areas where women are located.

As a consequence, young boys are not being raised to learn how to be comfortable with and respectful to women in public. They are raised to think of themselves almost as predators who cannot be trusted, and then when brutal things happen against women, there is almost a sense of acceptance. A most extreme example of this for me is the story about the female CBS 60-Minutes News reporter, Lara Logan, in 2011 who was mauled and sexually attacked in Cairo's Tahrir Square during the Arab Spring.[xi] This incident really bothered me, especially since, as a student in Cairo in the early 1980's, I recalled being rudely touched and poked whenever I was in a crowd. I remember thinking, what was wrong with these boys that they thought they had the right to do this in public? Logan, you may recall, in 2011, was separated from her crew, and some 200 to 300 Egyptian men molested her until an Egyptian woman, cloaked in her black *abayya*, managed to drag her away. How could society not hold these boys responsible for their actions against a woman who was there to do her job? Aren't Arab boys learning that this is entirely inappropriate behavior? Certainly, this is an area where women across the Arab world can do more as mothers in raising their sons to take responsibility for their actions and to respect women. Men in this part of the world need to grow up learning they can be trustworthy individuals who can deal respectfully with women, especially now that there are so many women who must carry out their jobs in public, more than ever before.

When I walked in the shopping malls alone in my western clothing in Kuwait, I would notice the very young Kuwaiti boys with their mothers covered in black staring at me. I had no idea what they were thinking or whether they really were even noticing me. The thought would cross my mind, though, whether they might be possibly thinking I was doing something wrong, something different from what they were being taught at home. I wondered if these young boys would grow up expecting all women in their lives to cover in public. Would they accept and respect women who did not cover? Certainly, they will one day go to school, and possibly even be educated overseas, where they will be exposed to the cultural reality that the world is a very diverse place and that not all women cover.

For now, many of these young Muslim boys are growing up in households where covering is the norm. I believe Kuwaitis are taught to be open-minded, but the truth is, an awful lot rests on how mothers decide to explain the world to their sons. Mothers and their young sons enjoy a special relationship as the loving Kuwaiti mom who told me, as she was about to leave the house one day, that her young son called to her, "*Mommy, don't forget your hijab! I don't want anyone to see how pretty you are!*" Another Kuwaiti mom wearing a deeply cut dress at a women's gathering commented proudly that her young son had scolded her before she left for wearing such a dress. Who knows what the impact will be on the type of relationships these young men will have with women in the future? Will these young boys prevent their own wives' beauty from being seen outside the home in public? What will their expectations be for their daughters?

In general, it is best for westerners to be mindful and respectful of local Kuwaiti customs and traditions when it comes to clothes. Women in particular need to be aware of Kuwaiti cultural preferences if they want to be accepted. Making sure shoulders, chests, and thighs are covered goes a long way. But in Kuwait, it is not always clear how far you need to go because there are so many Kuwaitis who dress the way they please. You simply can not know for sure when you crossed the line. One of our female officers at the embassy, a striking redhead, told me how she had misjudged how her sundress would be received at the stylish mile-long mall known as *The Avenues*. She had thought she had taken the appropriate precaution by tying a scarf around her neck to cover her chest. After all, she had seen other women wearing sundresses but this time apparently, her efforts were not enough. A mall security officer, who was wearing his *dishdasha*, decided her shoulders were too exposed. He pulled her aside and told her she could not enter unless she covered them.[xii]

Diplomats should always be conscious about what is deemed socially correct, especially if they want to be in the press to promote their events. When we held events at our residence and invited the press, I had to take care not to be seen holding a glass of wine since alcohol was forbidden in the country. Sometimes the press decided to take matters in its own hands when it came to potential social taboos. For instance, when the lovely wife of the German ambassador wore her German *dirndl* dress with the traditional bodice, low-cut blouse, full skirt and apron for Germany's National Day celebration, the press simply painted a less revealing blouse onto her photo. She appeared in the Kuwaiti papers the next day as the perfect hostess.[xiii]

More concerning then dress, however, a Kuwaiti mother told me she had decided to pull her son from a co-educational school and put him in a school only for boys. She did not think he should be around girls from outside the family. I wondered how he was going to learn how to mix with girls, and later young women, on a broader scale? I thought about whether conservative Islamic women weren't the ones who might actually help perpetuate the Arab world's acknowledgement of the "nature of women."Perhaps it is the mothers of today who will ensure that traditional society will remain as it is into the future. Many women in Kuwait, it seemed, were raising their sons to fulfill this destiny. My hope is that they also raise their sons to deal with women appropriately in all situations, however they dress.

Understandably, the overwhelming numbers of foreigners who have come to their country since the discovery of oil have caused Kuwaitis to seek to preserve their cultural identity. Reminding people in the country to respect their religion and traditions is a way for Kuwaitis to assert control over their country. Every now and then expats are made aware if there is something they are doing that is not consistent with

Kuwait's identity. Perhaps this is also why so many Kuwaitis prefer to distinguish themselves by wearing their traditional dress in Kuwait. Kuwaiti men often wear their *dishdashas* as a signal to others that they are Kuwaiti citizens to avoid being mistaken as foreigners themselves.[xiv] With nearly three-quarters of Kuwait's population classified as foreign citizens,[xv] it is not surprising that Kuwaitis also find relative safety and comfort in wearing their traditional clothing in public. In the same way men wear their *dishdashas*, many Kuwaiti women wear their conservative black *abayyas* as a symbol of their status as Kuwaitis. Their *abayyas* are a message to foreign men in particular that they are off limits. [xvi]

Through the prism of my western eyes, it was initially very hard for me to understand the concept of covering and gender separation when I first arrived in Kuwait, but I have come to accept these as cultural norms in Kuwait today. I have come to learn that Kuwaiti women are very proud to wear the veil and enjoy the privileges accorded to them by acting in concert with their religious and traditional values. A couple of Kuwaiti female engineers who cover told me they were so pleased with their personal accomplishments in both their careers and families that they wanted the world to know that Kuwaiti women, including those who veil, have the ability to achieve whatever they want. I have to admire and respect this.

Eventually I met wives of important Kuwaiti officials. The Foreign Minister's wife, Sheikha Aida, for example, accompanied her husband to the Foreign Ministry's special late night meal held during Ramadan. It was so great of her to come since all the ambassadors and their spouses were in attendance. I had also seen Sheikha Aida take on a very public role at the Bayan Palace several months earlier. As the chairwoman of the board of the Sheikh Salim Al-Ali Al-Sabah Informatics Award, she presented American engineer Steven J. Sasson, the inventor of the digital camera, with the 14th Edition of the Informatics Award in December 2014. It occurred to me that I was invited to this palace event because she was the one presenting. The following year, she gave the same award to

Bill Gates. I was fortunate to have also been invited to a dinner in his honor at the Shuwaikh Palace, the home of Sheikh Nasser Mohammed Ahmad Al-Jaber Al-Sabah, an important ruling family member and former prime minister. Sitting at that grand honorary banquet table for Bill Gates with a hundred or so people in attendance, is one experience as wife of the U.S. Ambassador in Kuwait that I will not forget.

Sheikha Aida is one of a few of the female members of the ruling family I met who chose to cover her hair; many others, however, did not. The ruling family seems to err on the side of modernity, and I admired their skill in maneuvering through the challenges posed by the push for greater religious conservatism in the country.

I came to Kuwait thinking it would be a relatively progressive country because women drive, work, and have the right to vote. True, but I also found gender relations far more complicated than I had imagined. Although many Kuwaiti women said they felt empowered by their religion, there were plenty of others in Kuwait concerned about the conservative and religious direction their country has taken. Some explain this new conservatism as a way to preserve Kuwait's identity in a fast-changing world. Others say it started with the 1979 Islamic Revolution in Iran or blame the religious fervor emanating from nearby Saudi Arabia. Whatever the case, I realized I was not expected to live under the same rules as Kuwaiti women. As an American woman and wife of a U.S. ambassador, I had the prerogative to be out and about in Kuwait as much as I wanted. And so, that was what I did. I simply got out there and participated.

My husband had tried to tell me from the beginning that I would be welcome wherever I went in Kuwait. But I had to find this out for myself first and feel comfortable. A year later, as I sat in the front row with my husband attending a youth entrepreneurship seminar, the Minister of Information and Minister of State for Youth Affairs Salman Sabah Al-Salem Al-Homoud Al-Sabah smiled as he shook my hand. He noted he had seen me around town quite a lot and seemed delighted that I had taken an interest in his country. At our second National Day celebration at the U.S. embassy on December 8, 2015, I was sure to be on stage with the kind and very tall Foreign Minister of Kuwait, Sabah Al Khaled Al Sabah. He was our official guest that year and together, with my husband, we cut the cake commemorating U.S.-Kuwaiti friendship with the stroke of a long ceremonial sword. I had found my way in Kuwait.

# CHAPTER FIVE

## *Gender Segregation and Educated Women*

Islamist activists have had a significant influence in Kuwait's educational arena over the past few decades and this includes the institutionalization of gender separation in the higher public education system. A law was passed in the Kuwaiti National Assembly in 1996 making this official but it has taken years to be fully implemented. At best, gender segregation is a stroke of genius enabling thousands of women from tribal backgrounds in Kuwait to get out of the house, obtain an education, and work outside the home.[xvii] At worst, it is a way to control women, whom they meet, and with whom they spend their time when they are at university. [xviii] Those in the middle on this issue say students focus better in class when they are not distracted by the opposite sex. Needless to say, gender segregation while I was in Kuwait was a contested topic.

While efforts were being made to ensure equal access to the same quality classrooms, textbooks, facilities, and instructors for both sexes, the road to achieve this equilibrium has been rocky. It is expensive to provide the same level of education for both sexes; everything essentially needs to be duplicated. For the current generation, achieving parity for both sexes has not been fast enough; some women have felt caught in the middle. For instance, an enthusiastic 27-year-old employee in the Kuwait Oil Company (KOC) I met during my visit was very disappointed with the quality of instruction in the science program at Kuwait University when she attended classes there several years ago.

Having graduated from one of Kuwait's premier private coed high schools, this young professional confided that she had been skeptical from the beginning about Kuwait's largest public university adapting segregated education. While attending Kuwait University, she felt her female science classes were not as well funded as the classes for men. The all-male classes had better professors who provided a better education overall. In her experience, though several years ago, many of the women in her classes were not serious about studying science and she missed the challenge of studying with male students in the way she had experienced at her high school. These segregation laws are unlikely to disappear anytime soon, especially since a new campus is under construction to house Kuwait University that will provide separate campuses for men and women. The cost to accomplish this will be exorbitant. Although the ultimate objective is to provide equal opportunities for both sexes, only time will tell if resources will in fact be equally allocated.

Ironically, for those of us who see things through western eyes, Kuwaiti women have actually been the proponents of gender segregation at Kuwait's institutions of higher learning.[xix] Wearing the veil and segregating themselves from men helps safeguard their reputations as good Muslims, especially as they maneuver under watchful eyes of their relatives and acquaintances at university. Any social dalliances are sure to be reported back to their families. While they want to enjoy their days out of the house and obtain a good education at the same time, they do not want to jeopardize their chances for marriage to a son of a worthy Kuwaiti family. They cannot risk having contacts with men that might be misinterpreted and hurt their chances of marrying a man deemed appropriate for their families.

Though the policy of gender separation may seem draconian, in practice, it is not. There is no atmosphere of dark oppression on Kuwaiti university campuses. Women are not sealed off from men and it is not as though there is no interaction between the sexes on the campuses. There are still places to meet men at university outside the classroom and there are plenty of opportunities to impress friends with their youthful fashion trends. Women have also not given up their caprice and whimsy as young college students on campus. Under their *abayyas*, they still flaunt their individuality and fashion. As you walk across campus, you can see their trendy sneakers and jeans as well as their glamorous stilettos. New hijab styles are on display and attractively embellished black *abayyas* sparkle across the campus. Women on Kuwaiti college campuses do not see themselves as deprived. The veils provide them the cover to do pretty much as they please without attracting unwanted attention to themselves. There are also plenty of women on campus who do not cover; they wear western clothing and bare their beautiful hair. They are very much accepted and integrated into the student population. They must, however, abide by the gender segregation laws like everyone else, whether they like it or not. These more secular and western women are less structured or systematic in representing their views on campus. In contrast, the Islamist oriented women on campus are more organized. They are the women who have worked hard to institutionalize gender segregation.[xx]

These Islamist women succeeded in establishing gender separation on campus through their participation in various student organizations and unions. Many grew up as members of larger political, social, and religious networks that teach them how to organize to obtain what they want. I was introduced to one such network during my second *Ramadan* in Kuwait in 2016, when I was invited to attend the ladies' *diwaniyya* for an organization known as the Secretariat of

Women's Work. It is customary to visit *diwaniyyas* in Kuwait City after the *Iftar* meal that breaks the daylong fast and the prayer that follows, and so I arrived around 9:00 pm.

When I entered the headquarters of the Women's Secretariat, I was greeted by smiling and serene faces of all ages; some of the older women were dressed in black while the others wore festive kaftans and colorful headscarves for Ramadan. This was my first exposure to an Islamic women's social network active in charitable work as well as in promoting religious and traditional values in Kuwait. I had entered a sphere of Kuwaiti society that I had not previously known. Suddenly, I was in a holy realm of dedicated believers. The ambiance was gracious and inviting. The mood was joyful as they were also inaugurating their new headquarters building that was an impressive hall to hold their *diwaniyyas*. I was ushered in and crossed the shining floor to sit on one of the ornate chairs lined against the walls.

The Secretariat of Work is part of the Social Reform Society, the charity arm of Kuwait's Muslim Brotherhood, known in the country as the Islamic Constitutional Movement (ICM). In Kuwait, the ICM's Social Reform Society is a major charity organization. According to the Forbes Middle East website, the Society generated $93.6 million in total income in 2011, and spent over $81.3 million directly on charitable causes in 2014. Contributions went as far away as Yemen to provide famine relief and Syria to help the refugees. At home, the society funded social development projects for local youth and women as well as for others in need.[xxi]

This Muslim charitable society, along with its political umbrella organization, the ICM, has helped establish many of the conservative social policies we see in Kuwait today, including policies like gender segregation in the higher education system.[xxii] Together with other Islamist and Salafist organizations, their organized efforts to elect Islamist parliamentarians have enabled Islamists to pass a number of laws upholding conservative religious practices, especially with regard to the role of women in society.[xxiii] The Women's

Secretariat mainly works behind the scenes, creating influential networks of grassroots support, and their female members do not generally seek public leadership roles.[xxiv] The women prefer to entrust political leadership, such as running for the National Assembly, to men while they focus their attention on family services. As a result, the children they reach and support tend to carry on the values of the organization into adult life, beginning in the universities.

The ladies at the Secretariat's *diwaniyya* were thrilled the wife of the American ambassador attended their event. As for me, I had so many questions, I could barely contain myself. I tried to strike up as many conversations as I could, first in Arabic, and then eventually finding people willing to converse with me in English. Several talked about what they did at their Society, about how they were especially focused on helping teach young girls to be responsible, educated, and successful women. One woman explained how the organization was especially focused on building strong families. Recognizing the high divorce rate in Kuwait, they taught young girls how to manage money and not to let disagreements about it tear their marriages apart. And because social media is so integral in Kuwaiti society, the organization taught young girls how to use it properly. I can imagine the Islamist women were concerned that women did not expose too much of themselves on the Internet. Their message seems to have had an effect. At women's wedding celebrations, for example, cell phones and picture-taking are strongly discouraged, and phones and cameras are sometimes even taken at the door. Women at these segregated affairs do not cover and often look particularly glamorous, too beautiful and attractive to be seen in public by the opposite sex.

Another woman I spoke with at the Secretariat talked about how the Society's work was helping fill the void created by so many Kuwaiti women working outside the home today. The Society provides children with after-school activities and tutoring. These ladies felt strongly about supporting career moms who needed a place for their kids after school to provide care and help with their homework. The Society was providing much needed services for Kuwait's many career women struggling with the demands of their work places as well as their homes. Of course, this is also a good way to win the allegiance of Kuwait's working mothers. During the summer, not surprisingly, the Islamist groups also provide educational camps for children. I recall hearing a story from a European ambassador in Kuwait about how his Kuwaiti friend from a liberal merchant family was sending his children to one of these summer camps. The friend explained there were no other camps and his wife was pulling her hair out for help in managing the kids. The family had no choice but to send their children to the Islamist camps. Islamist organizations in Kuwait, as in other countries across the Middle East, are providing much-needed social services not provided by either the government or the private sector.

Younger members of the Secretariat also attended the *diwaniyya*. One told me she had just completed her freshman year at college in Colorado where she was preparing to study to become an engineer. Her plan was to transfer universities and attend the Colorado School of Mines. She was looking forward to returning to the States, but expressed concern about how Americans would view her hijab if then-presumptive Republican nominee, Donald Trump, became President. She was responding to all the media hype about his rhetoric concerning Muslims and immigration in June 2016. I assured her she should return to the States, study hard, and follow her dreams.

As I was leaving, a young girl at the door proudly told me how her brothers were studying in the States. Then she looked down and said her father would not let her go. She looked sad, but then broke into a bright smile when she expressed hope that one day she would have the same opportunity as her brothers to study in America. Her father said he might allow her to pursue an advanced degree there. I left thinking all was not perfect for members of this organization and that not everyone's interest was being served.

I visited the Secretariat again for its reception to celebrate Eid al-Fitr, marking the end of Ramadan's month-long period of fasting and introspection. This time I was able to chat with one of the women involved directly in some of the political efforts of the Secretariat. This woman, in her fifties, was a lawyer familiar with the ICM's political agenda. She seemed happy to talk to me, as she highlighted three areas her organization was focusing on as of 2016. One objective was to oppose the United Nations efforts to overcome violence and discrimination against people on the basis of their sexual orientation and gender identity in Kuwait.[xxv] She mentioned her organization had even spoken with conservative Christian organizations in the United States about how to counter gay rights in the political arena. In her view, gay rights undermined the institution of the family and her organization was determined to oppose any changes in Kuwaiti laws. She was unabashed about her organization's resolve to discriminate on the basis of sexual orientation and gender identification, despite international conventions that call for protecting universal human rights enshrined by the United Nations.

Another goal she mentioned was to ensure that certain Shi'a books would not be allowed in Kuwait. She did not provide the names of these books but she believed them to be dangerous and heretical, adding that the books were attempts by Iran to undermine the State of Kuwait. When I pointed out that Kuwait's Shi'a population was 30 percent and that they had rights too, she retorted that the 30 percent figure was inaccurate. She asserted that Kuwait's Shi'a population was closer to 15 percent based on voting records. Current statistics available on Kuwait's population census maintain, however, that as many as a third of the population are Shi'a. Despite her efforts to downplay the presence of Shi'a in the country, her organization believed it had the right to squelch freedom of religion and expression in the name of national security. This position is indicative of the dangers present in fanning the flames of sectarianism in the country. Given Kuwait's proximity to Iran, however, there is some justification for concern over attempts by Iran to gain influence over Kuwait's population.

Lastly, she talked about how her party was organizing to oppose any change to laws requiring Kuwaiti women between the ages 15 and 25 to have their marriages sanctioned by male guardians. As far as her organization was concerned, it was important for senior male members of the family to have control over their daughters' marriages. Families could not risk having their daughters marry into families of which they did not approve or did not trust to protect their own family's interests. The problem is that prohibiting a young adult woman into her 20's from deciding whom she should marry is discriminatory. The Kuwaiti practice of controlling their daughters' marriages into adulthood violates women's rights. Advocates for international human rights are thus urging the Kuwaiti government to lower the age requiring male approval to enable adult women to have the freedom to marry whom they choose.

Naively, I had thought this female activist would have been more interested in promoting women's rights. I thought her agenda would reflect the interests of the highly educated Kuwaiti women I had been meeting who now not only had advanced degrees but were financially independent with professional careers. Instead, her political efforts revolved around issues that would help men retain control over the institution of the family. It seems to me that while Kuwaiti women have the power to put their country at the forefront of achieving women's right in the Gulf region, the large number of Islamist women in Kuwait have decided that it is more important to preserve the traditional family structure. In their mind, it is more useful to focus on helping women achieve success in their careers and in raising their families. Issues that concern them include maternity leave, childcare, and other work friendly policies; they are also increasingly active in supporting home-based jobs and pressing for opportunities to work part-time and have flexible hours so they can continue to work while raising children.[xxvi] They value their separate incomes because they know it gives them greater independence, especially in cases of divorce, or worse, death of their spouses. And yet they defer to men to focus their political energy in society by choosing not to be front and center in the Parliament.

This generation of Islamist women has grown up understanding the role of political activism in society and as they ascertain more about women's issues both inside and outside the home, I am hoping they will be motivated to ameliorate societal inequities that currently favor men in the Gulf region. Their success as accomplished Muslim women in Kuwait has not gone unnoticed, especially on social media. Women all over the Gulf, including in Saudi Arabia, are well aware of the privileges enjoyed by Kuwaiti women.[xxvii] In fact, when Kuwaiti women voted for the first time in 2006, authorities in Saudi Arabia sealed their borders because they did not want Saudi women to see that Kuwaiti women were voting.[xxviii] Now Saudi women know what Kuwaiti women are doing through social media, and many want what Kuwaiti women already have. They want to drive, hold public office, and work outside the home according to tweets boldly posted on their Twitter accounts.[xxix]

Education has raised the status of women in Kuwait, and the region knows that Kuwaiti women enjoy a greater degree of gender equality. In Kuwait, women and men are guaranteed free and equal access to education from primary school through university.[xxx] At the university level, women comprise almost two-thirds of the student body. This high figure, however, can also be attributed to the large number of male students who study outside Kuwait, leaving women to fill the ranks of the higher education institutions in Kuwait. Nonetheless, it is significant so many women are attending Kuwait University, especially since the acceptance rate is quite competitive.

I have met several women who have told me they did not get into Kuwait University because their GPA was not high enough. One explained that she simply did not want to work hard during her senior year in high school because she was feeling "lazy" and so she had a C+ average. She did not get accepted to Kuwaiti University, but this did not deter her from pursuing higher education. In Kuwait, there are a number of options to pursue an education, including studying at any one of the private colleges that have sprouted in Kuwait like the Gulf University for Science and Technology and the American University in Kuwait. They can also study abroad; but for those who do not have high GPA's, they will not have the advantage of receiving generous scholarships from the government.

My point is that women have opportunities for education at every step of the way, and this has greatly empowered them in Kuwait. Their exposure to so much knowledge in the world and their obvious sophistication make me wonder if they will also want eventually to achieve total gender equality in society, especially when it comes to the laws of the land. Only time will tell. It is safe to say though, that women in Kuwait are well placed to make the move if they wish, especially if the region can lay to rest the menacing threat of ISIS and other radical elements trying to gain power and influence.

# CHAPTER SIX

## *Leaning Conservative*

The increased radicalism in the region with the rise of ISIS in 2014, resulting for the first time in the establishment of a caliphate in part of nearby Iraq, almost certainly put Kuwaiti society on edge. It was no wonder people were choosing to lean more conservatively. Many Kuwaitis believed that by behaving more conservatively, they would not attract the ire of radical entities across their borders. But fear of the radicals could not alone explain why Kuwait had become more conservative. Nor could this simply be attributed to Muslims becoming more faithful to their religion. The last few decades have been marked by a turn inward in the region, and for many people there, this has meant a revival of their faith in Islam. However, social conservatism was also adopted as a reaction to the rapid modernity brought on by so much oil wealth and exposure to the west. Clearly the conservative trend in the region was a complex issue but I wanted to know more about it. I wanted to understand why so many women in the region had abandoned western fashion for the veil.

Once oil was discovered in the first half of the 20th century, many Kuwaitis embraced the westernization and modernity that came with development of this prized resource. Kuwaiti merchant families in particular rushed to send their sons abroad for education so they could take part in this newly discovered world of riches and culture. The merchant families also began sending their daughters abroad to study as early as the 1950's.[xxxi] This group of women became the first generation to go to university. They studied in Cairo and Beirut and in places as far away as Britain and the United States. They mostly studied without their veils, and their families grew accustomed to seeing them without being covered when they visited or returned home. According to Kuwaiti historian Haya al-Mughni, these women had no desire to wear the *abayya* once they returned to Kuwait, even if it meant not being able to work.[xxxii] According to al-Mughni, the educated women came to see the veil as backward and didn't think it was fair that they had to wear it in order to work for the government. Their families agreed and supported their daughters and exerted pressure on the government to change. Kuwaitis who also wanted to modernize the country joined in and by 1961, the government agreed to give women permission to work without wearing veils. Emboldened, women also began wearing the latest western fashions, including miniskirts.[xxxiii] Their new jobs provided income, and they enjoyed a sense of independence never felt before. They could afford to buy the things they wanted and even drive their own cars where they needed to go. The sixties and seventies brought the women's liberation movement all the way from the United States and the European continent to Kuwait's door.

Older Kuwaitis like to reminisce about the time when women wore miniskirts and other western fashions in public. In National Geographic's May 1969 article, "Kuwait, Aladdin's Lamp of the Middle East," the authors actually referred to the *abayya* and *hijab* as a "fading fashion" and published a photograph of a covered woman in full *niqab* describing her as a "rarity." The caption read, "Robe and veil have been cast aside except by the most conservative women, who seldom leave their homes." While the traditional veil may have been "cast aside" by women of the merchant class who lived in the city, they were still very much a part of the lives of the tribal and Bedouin women who lived on the outskirts. The National Geographic authors just did not happen to see these women.

The merchant class dominated the city in these years, and they were more amenable to the western lifestyle brought in by the many expats arriving with the oil boom. Lore has it that Kuwait had the most amazing social life, including parties with alcohol. There were even a number of nightclubs in town, like the famous "Gazelle Club."[xxxiv] This was a place where bands like "The Sheila Carter Band" played while expats and Kuwaitis enjoyed music and dancing late into the night. An expat blog remembered the Gazelle Club fondly as a place to have "plenty of fresh fruit, seafood, and all the booze one could ever want."[xxxv] The Gazelle Club was destroyed by the Iraqis during the 1990 invasion and was never rebuilt. Many say that the invasion marked the end of the free-spirited Kuwait captured in the 1969 National Geographic article. The glamorous nightlife in Kuwait prior to the war, I am told, has never really returned.

Although Kuwaiti authorities banned alcohol in an act of parliament in 1964, the law was not strictly enforced before the 1990 invasion. Alcohol is forbidden in Islam, and conservatives in the Kuwaiti government felt increasingly obliged to implement the law more aggressively, especially in the post-liberation era beginning in 1991. Today no bars can be found in hotels, nor can wine or beer be served at restaurants. Although many Kuwaitis still offer alcoholic drinks in the privacy of their homes, alcohol has become more difficult to obtain and very expensive.

A European expat told me in December 2015 that a bottle of scotch on the black market could be as much as $200, more if it was particularly high quality.[xxxvi] The acquaintance said he was reconciled to the extra cost, since he did not pay taxes and enjoyed subsidized gas, water, and other utilities that were at the time provided by the government. On the other hand, this European expat was wise, explaining that although he was earning a half million-dollar salary as a senior manager in the food business, he was careful not to squander it. He knew his position was not going to last forever. Many expats come to Kuwait, he said, and lose their senses with the sudden increase in their salaries. They rent expensive penthouse apartments, go on incredible vacations, drive fancy sports cars, and procure expensive bottles of wine and other libations. They find their money goes pretty quickly. If they are lucky, their jobs in Kuwait continue; if they are not, they go back to their countries with little to show. There are no guarantees for expats who come to Kuwait and try to live the high life.

While strictly banning alcohol in public reflects the Islamic trend in the country, it is also indicative of the conservative Bedouin culture that began seeping into the city by the 1980's. Kuwaiti society can be divided along a single fault line; on one side, there are the settled people, the *hadar*, and the other are the nomadic people, the *Bedu*. While the merchant families (*hadar*) were comfortable with the many new luxuries and bon vivant lifestyles penetrating the country in the oil boom, Kuwaitis from the Bedouin tribes (nomads) along the borders of Saudi Arabia and Iraq were not.

Eventually, a decade after the National Geographic 1969 article was written, Bedouin families began to move to the city so they too could enjoy the benefits of an oil economy and the growing welfare state.[xxxvii] But once they started arriving, they brought their tribal culture, their patriarchal hierarchy where men earned the money and led the family. Women, meanwhile, remained at home to raise the children and take care of the house. Their presence would eventually reverse the progressive movement that had been ushered in by the west and embraced by the merchant families.

Soon, the Bedouin families also began to prosper from their newly acquired government jobs, subsidized utilities, and social services including a free education and medical care. Female members were permitted to participate in their promising new urban life as long as they were under the cover of a veil. Family honor still remained paramount even though they were no longer living in tents in the desert. If their daughters were to benefit from the opportunities afforded by the government, they would have to do so in a way that that would not shame the family. Gradually, as Bedouin women adapted to their new urban lives, more and more veils appeared on the streets of Kuwait City. The veil was their most reliable tactic to get out of the house and participate in public life. For them, the veil offered freedom and opportunity beyond what they had ever imagined, including an education and a job.

Not all the Bedouin arriving in the urban centers were Kuwaiti. Many Bedouins arriving on Kuwait's borders were from neighboring Saudi Arabia and Iraq. They began forming shantytowns on the outskirts of the city, waiting to join the labor force or possibly obtain the coveted Kuwaiti citizenship. There was also plenty of other migrant labor in the shantytowns that arrived from Lebanon, Palestine, and Syria who were not Bedouin.[xxxviii] For the Kuwaiti government, the question became how to determine the legal status of so many gathering on their borders. For those arriving from the nomadic tribes of Iraq and Saudi Arabia, it was difficult to ascertain their connection to current Kuwaiti citizens. It was difficult to know when exactly they arrived or where were they from. It was hard to be sure what tribe they belonged and whether they could be trusted to be loyal and worthy citizens. After independence in 1961, the Kuwaiti government felt it needed to have more specific rules regarding who would receive the prized Kuwaiti citizenship.[xxxix]

It was decided that only those who could prove they had ancestors in Kuwait before 1920 could become citizens. This was the year Wahhabi tribes loyal to Ibn Saud attacked the protective wall of Kuwait at the Battle of Jahra in an attempt to take territory controlled by the Al-Sabah family. It is a battle that has not been forgotten in Kuwait, because if they had lost, their territory might have been absorbed under Ibn Saud's rule and ultimately into the Kingdom of Saudi Arabia. Using the year 1920 as a guidepost, Kuwait gave citizenship to some 220,000 people between 1965 and 1981.[xl] Many new guest workers, however, arriving well after 1920 also managed to become citizens during this time. The ruling family needed to increase Kuwait's population to provide manpower for its police and military and decided to recruit from the Bedouin population on the borders. Initially few of these new migrant labors, however, were given the right to vote.[xli] Later, as the ruling family became concerned with the balance of power vis-à-vis the powerful merchant families in Kuwait City, it began to extend voting rights in the 1960's and 70's to some of the newly naturalized Bedouin tribes. The objective was that the new Bedouin migrants would vote for members of parliament who would challenge the increasing power of the merchant families.[xlii]

Many of these Bedouin tribes came from Saudi Arabia, and they brought with them an affinity for the very conservative branch of Islam known as *Wahhabism*. This branch of Islam that is distinctly from Saudi Arabia emphasized strict adherence to the words of Islam's holy book, the *Qur'an*, and the *Sunnah*, the teachings of the Prophet Muhammad and his followers. *Wahhabism* played an important role in uniting the tribes on the Arabian Peninsula when Ibn Saud, the first monarch and founder of the Kingdom of Saudi Arabia in 1932, embraced its teachings. This branch of Islam, founded by Muhammad Ibn 'Abd Al-Wahhab in the 18th century, appealed to Arabian tribes for its compatibility with desert customs.[xliii] According to a successful Kuwaiti businessman from the merchant class, Wahhabism was not present in Kuwait prior to the arrival of these Saudi tribes.[xliv]

Well before Saudi tribes and other outsiders became citizens of Kuwait, Kuwait had adopted its constitution in 1961 based on Egyptian Civil Code and *Shari'a* law derived from the *Maliki* School of Islamic jurisprudence. *Maliki* law allows for greater flexibility, including personal opinion and consensus, and recognizes supplementary sources of law as well.[xlv] There are four primary Sunni schools of jurisprudence, including the Hanafi, Shafi'i, Maliki and Hanbali rites. The *Hanbali* School of Islamic jurisprudence forms the basis of *Wahhabism* and is also the school that is officially followed by Saudi Arabia and also

Qatar. Unlike the Maliki School, the Hanbali School rejects human reason in all forms as a source of law and insists that each and every legal rule find its requisite authority in the divine revelation of the Qur'an and the practice of example of the Prophet.[xlvi] In fact, according to N. J. Coulson in his book, *A History of Islamic Law*, the founder of the Hanbali School, Ahmad ibn-Hanbal, "was alleged to have never eaten watermelon because he was not in possession of any Prophetic precedent on the subject." The fact that Kuwait did not choose to follow the Hanbali School suggests that this ultra conservative Islam was not as influential in Kuwait prior to the arrival of tribes from Saudi Arabia.

Today, many of Kuwait's conservative Islamists describe themselves as *Salafis*, rather than *Wahabbis* as they do not want to show any allegiance to the Saudi brand. Both, however, advocate very strict and similar interpretations of Islam. Salafism in Kuwait attracts a broad following, appealing to Kuwaiti Muslims who advocate a return to Islamic order with greater adherence to Shari'a law including severe punishment for crimes and disobedience. The Salafi litany of taboos including alcohol, smoking, singing, listening to music, dancing, wearing silk, wearing ornaments of gold or silver, and drawing and painting animate objects, to name a few, have become familiar platforms of those who follow this austere branch of Islam.

As Bedouins who espoused Salafist ideas began populating urban spaces in Kuwait, they also began lobbying Kuwaiti politicians and involving themselves in the democratic parliamentary process. They obtained jobs in ministries with high social impact like the Ministry of Education and Ministry of Awqaf (Religious Endowments) and Islamic Affairs.[xlvii] By the 1990's, Islamists had succeeded in implementing more conservative laws and giving a more conservative character to the city. Eventually, miniskirts disappeared, nightclubs closed, and veils were back in vogue. Salafi strength was demonstrated most profoundly when Islamists succeeded in winning the majority of parliamentary seats in elections held in 1992 and 1996.[xlviii]

Perhaps this is why music and dance have become less public in Kuwait and therefore more difficult to come by. For instance, it is difficult to hire a DJ to play western music in hotels or other public venues. Permission has to be obtained from the Kuwaiti government, and authorities retain the right to shut down music when performed in public at any time. The American Women's League (AWL) managed to receive such permission and a DJ was present for its special Valentine's Day event in 2016 held at a local hotel. It wasn't long before the mainly American and other expat attendees were up and dancing to the music. Hotel security quickly shut the music down after complaints were received from hotel guests. My husband and I attended this event and had left before this happened, but not without having danced to a few tunes and noticing how much fun everyone was having.

In the newspaper, not long after, I read about an Arab entertainer reprimanded by the Ministry of Information for his spontaneous dancing on Kuwait television during an interview with a local female TV personality. The Ministry noted that the entertainer's behavior ran counter to the "rules and disciplines of Kuwait TV which is a safe haven to the society."[xlix] Dancing in public is a serious issue and Kuwaiti authorities are not shy about making their views known when challenged. When our embassy staff invited a visiting U.S. Army rock band to play for a large crowd at the outdoor theater in Shaheed Park, they also ran into trouble. After coordinating the event with Kuwait's Ministry of Interior to ensure security for the show, it was soon apparent that Kuwaiti authorities were also concerned there might be dancing during the concert. So, when one of the singers in the band on stage was about to invite the audience to dance, our embassy officers in the front row frantically waved the idea down. But it was too late. A music loving Kuwaiti, in a *dishdasha* no less, was already lost to the beat of the music. When he stood up to dance, he was immediately surrounded by security and told to sit down.[l]

Despite consternation about music and dance in public, Kuwait has built the enormous Sheikh Jaber Al-Ahmed Cultural Center that contains a number of brand new state-of-the-art theaters. This spectacular modern complex sits along Kuwait City's Gulf shore in four separate polygon shapes wrapped in titanium. They appear as if they were meteors dropped from the sky. These impressive theaters opened in 2016, and it will be interesting to see how successful this ambitious project will be. The venue is perfect for bringing to Kuwait top international stars, in the same way world-class entertainers perform in Dubai and Muscat. But one has to wonder what sort of restrictions the Kuwaitis will impose should these entertainers perform here. Although Kuwait is not in the same league as Saudi Arabia in terms of conservatism, it does sometimes act like it is. There are many conservative Islamists in Kuwait who have been influenced by the more austere Salafi teachings from Saudi Arabia who believe music is *haram*, forbidden, because music, according to Salafis, can lead people into a trance that might lead them to do things they shouldn't.[li]

It is difficult to know whether Kuwait will encourage more western entertainment and its many trappings to come into their country. Music, singing, dancing and clapping hands together have long been very important in Kuwaiti life, especially when people worked hard to make their living from the sea.[lii] During long voyages, Kuwaiti musicians would sing to help the crew move their oars to a melodic rhythm in unison.[liii] At night they would play music and sing to pass the time.

Kuwait is not alone in the spread of Islamic fundamentalism; it can be found around the world. It is today present in Muslim majority countries in Asia, Africa, and throughout the Middle East, thanks in large part to Saudi charitable contributions in the form of building of mosques and schools.[liv] When I asked a sincerely religious *muhajibah* (a woman who covers) who is also a senior official in an international organization about whether I should be concerned that Saudi Arabia has helped spread this highly restrictive brand of Islam around the world, she said she was very angry about this, to the point that she would not even travel to Saudi Arabia, even to make the *hajj*.[lv] She believes that the extremist propagation of the faith has given Islam an unnecessarily bad image around the world. With their home court advantage, conservative Islamists in Saudi Arabia have long been able to propagate their strict brand to the millions of Muslim pilgrims (hajjis) who transit Saudi Arabia each year to pray at the Holy Cities of Mecca and Medina.[lvi] The global presence of Saudi-financed mosques and schools have also contributed to the spread of this conservative brand of Islam around the world.

Kuwaiti Salafists, however, do not dominate their country's diverse population. The large number of Shi'a in the country, around 30 percent of the Kuwaiti population, in itself suggests that the ultra-conservative Sunni population cannot possibly represent the majority of Kuwaitis. There are also many liberal Sunni merchant families in Kuwait who do not support these hardline Sunni Islamists. It is just that the conservative Islamists in Kuwait tend to be more organized and purposeful, and have succeeded in being very influential in the society. For the liberals, the influence of these Islamists is extremely troubling. They are particularly concerned about how this strict and narrow form of Islam has penetrated the core of their nation and has even reached into their children's textbooks.

A friend once complained how she was fed up with the way her children were learning Arabic in school, frustrated with the conservative curriculum adopted by the Ministry of Education. She reminisced how she loved to study Arabic when she was a girl, because she would learn about the world in her classes reading books and newspapers. Now her children's Arabic language curriculum is much changed, more restricted to topics about the Arab culture and religion. In frustration, she asked, "Haven't we progressed beyond nomads searching for water in the desert? Don't we have more serious problems to consider?" Arabic classes are today more focused on preparing kids to memorize the Qur'an rather than learn about international affairs through newspapers and other media.

Another acquaintance explained that when he went to school in the 1970's, his Palestinian and Egyptian teachers taught verses of Pre-Islamic (*Jahiliyya*, meaning "ignorance") poetry in Arabic literature class, beautiful stories like the love affair between a young Bedouin girl named Abla and a young Bedouin boy named Antar. Now, only verses from the Qur'an are used as examples of Arabic poetry in his children's classes. He admitted that most of the Qur'an's verses are poetic, but lamented the implied view that there was nothing worthwhile to learn about Arab culture before the advent of Islam.

I reviewed one of the Ministry of Education's Arabic language primers used during the 2014-2015 school year for foreign high school students. It was the book my son used in his introductory class during his senior year at the American School of Kuwait. The pictures in the textbook were very old-fashioned. The boys were shown playing soccer, and the girls were not seen doing much except smiling and being happy. There were a couple of pictures of women in the kitchen or working as teachers but beyond that, there were no other role models for young girls. The last chapter of the book was dedicated to vocabulary used for praying in the mosque, with pictures showing only a group of boys praying. Several parents voiced their concern about the messages their children were receiving from these socially conservative, old-fashioned textbooks depicting a fictitious life from 1950's.

A Kuwaiti acquaintance in the ruling family put it bluntly when she summed up the situation describing the wave of Islamic conservatism in the country. In her analysis, the strong conservative expression of the Islamic faith today was actually a push for power by those who wish to use the religion to achieve political control. She described the effort as another "ism", much like socialism, communism, and nationalism. She called this particular "ism", "Islamism." [lvii] Islamism, as many

Muslims argue, is not Islam. Islamism is not a faith; it is a political agenda that is not indigenous to Kuwait but rather imported from Egypt and Saudi Arabia. Although its appearance in Kuwait began before Saddam Hussein's invasion, in the decades since, it has taken hold and spread.[lviii] In her view, Islamism will one day also pass; not the religion of course, just the very conservative expression we see today. Islamism will pass in the way that socialism and communism have passed, she argued.

She has a point. There are certainly political undertones in the rise of religious conservatism in Kuwait, and there is a history of "isms" in the region. The political winds that breezed through the Middle East in the 1950's, 60's, and 70's saw the rise and fall of momentous secular political experiments like Arab social**ism** and pan-Arab**ism**. These movements were brought into Kuwait as the personal convictions of the Palestinians, Egyptians, Lebanese, and Syrians who arrived as expat laborers. Egyptians, for example, were very attracted to the idea of socialism as a way to redistribute wealth. Before Gamal Abdel Nasser led the military coup that overthrew Egypt's monarchy in 1952, less than half of one percent of all Egyptians owned more than a third of all fertile land.[lix] Once in power, Nasser nationalized the country's land and resources as a way to redistribute wealth. I still remember sitting on a plane to Cairo in 1979 next to an expatriate Egyptian woman who lived in Europe and her story about how her family lost practically all their wealth due to Nasser. Her family had moved to Paris but of course never forgot what happened to them. Socialism would eventually fade, but not before Egypt's charismatic Nasser popularized his ideological secular brand of Arab nationalism.

Arab nationalism urged Arabs from across the region to unite as one nation. The dream was for Arabs to come together on the basis of their common Arabic language and shared history. Their religious, ethnic, and national differences were to be set aside. Egypt rode the crest of this idealistic, pan-Arab wave and Nasser became the Arab world's most ardent proponent. Arabs from across the region espoused this idealist vision. In 1958, Nasser forged the United Arab Republic with Syria, but it fell apart by 1961 following a coup in Syria. Syria felt Egypt was trying to dominate so it broke from the union.

The political experiment of Arab unity quickly met its end following the Six-Day Arab-Israeli War in 1967. Israel not only won the war but also captured territory in Egypt's Sinai Peninsula, Jordan's West Bank, and Syria's Golan Heights. Palestinians multiplied as refugees and were left to depend on themselves to defend their cause. There was a great deal of Arab introspection after this humiliating defeat. It was about this time when many Arab Muslims in the region found solace and strength in their religion. The powerful and persuasive Muslim Brotherhood in Egypt began to attract more followers to its fundamentalist movement. Disillusioned Egyptians turned away from Nasser and his secular ideas. People in Egypt and in the region began to see Islam as the solution. As Egyptian and Levantine Arabs came to work in Kuwait in the 80's and 90's, Kuwaitis who were themselves advocates of Islamic fundamentalism welcomed them into the fold.

In his book, *The Arab Predicament*, Lebanese scholar Fouad Ajami cited a revealing questionnaire administered by a social scientist working at Kuwait University in 1977. Nearly five hundred undergraduates were asked about their views on Arab unity, family, state, and religion. The sample included students from nearly every Arab country who were studying at the university. The results of the survey highlighted the demise of pan-Arabism and the subsequent rise of Islamic influence. A large portion supported Islamic sentiment and patriotism for each individual Arab state. The dreams of Arab nationalism and unity were proven dead.[ix] The vacuum left behind by the death of secular ideologies like socialism and pan-Arabism was being filled by religious belief and loyalty to the state. In many ways, the questionnaire was a harbinger of the strong role Islam would play in the Arab world in the future.

As Kuwait witnessed the rising power of Sunni fundamentalism, it also had to withstand the pressures imposed by the ruling Shi'a theocracy that came to power in Tehran with the Iranian revolution in 1979. By the eighties, Iran succeeded in exporting its revolutionary ideas to Shi'a allies in Lebanon through its support of Lebanese Hezbollah. The U.S. embassy in Kuwait was bombed in 1983 by a group connected to them, led by famed terrorist mastermind, Imad Mughniyah. It is not an exaggeration to say that the hard-line stances taken by both Shi'a leaders in Iran and Sunni leaders in Saudi Arabia have caused great tension in sectarian relations in the past few decades. It is easy to see this tension in the destabilization occurring in many countries in the region including in Yemen, Syria, Lebanon, and Iraq. Many in the region can remember the days when no one made a big deal about religious differences and when both sects lived peacefully for generations. Inter-marrying within the sects was common place; it still happens today but only among the more liberal minded. Kuwait's ruling family has worked hard to avoid sectarian tensions occurring among their own people, and it is to their credit that Kuwait has succeeded in avoiding similar instability.

Kuwait is unique. It is blessed with enormous resources, and its relatively democratic government cares about the prosperity of its people. I have met many Kuwaitis who understand that if they work through their legitimate authorities rooted in their democratic institutions, their cultural structure, and religion, possibilities for progress and change are real. I think this is what a Kuwaiti social science professor at Kuwait University was trying to tell me one afternoon in 2015, though at the time I did not fully understood what he meant. He was trying to explain to me why his female assistant was wearing her hijab even though she did not particularly want to. He said she was doing it because her family and society were telling her to do it. He went on to say that if one day someone with religious credibility and legitimate authority rose up and said that it was no longer necessary for Muslim women to cover their hair, many Muslim women would no longer cover their hair.[lxi] Conformity and order enable Kuwaitis to navigate their society successfully and so change will likely only come under the guidance of an entity respected by all.

# CHAPTER SEVEN

## *Weddings the Kuwaiti Way*

In April 2015, Tamara Saab of the Tee and Aki morning radio show on Kuwait's Superstation 99.7 called our embassy to see if I was available to be the chief guest at a fashion show. *La Bourjoisie Fashion House* was going to show its 2015 bridal collection at the Hilton Hotel just south of Kuwait City. Of course, I was available! This sounded like a really fun thing to do. Talented Lebanese designers who established their fashion house in Kuwait in 2010 created the *La Bourjoisie* brand. American celebrities such as Britney Spears and Nicki Minaj, as well as Arab brides and entertainers from across the region, have worn their designs.[lxii]

But when I arrived at the hotel venue with the long runway jetting from the center of the room, I wondered at first whether I was in the right place. I had come alone that evening and found that I was the only westerner present. What I did not anticipate was that I would be watching the fashion show with a hundred or so women who were completely covered in black. They were all seated on either side of the runway, wearing their long black *abayyas* and veils. Some were also covering their faces with a *niqab* and wore long black gloves to cover their hands. I wondered what sort of fashion show this could possibly be if the audience was dressed in such modest attire.

My first reaction was to tug at my elbow-length sleeves to cover the rest of my arms. No one in the room, however, seemed the least bit concerned about how I was dressed. I was immediately welcomed and ushered to a comfortable front row seat. I waited with the rest of the women for the show to begin, sipping on colorful exotic fruit juices. When some of the women nearby learned that I was the wife of the U.S. ambassador, several wanted to take their pictures with me. They were happy to have me there. Tamara, an American of Lebanese Druze heritage, soon came over. She was not covered and wore a long, beautiful blue *La Bourjoisie* satin skirt with a long sleeved white silk blouse. She was the master of ceremonies for the evening and she looked stunning. She had no idea I had never been to an event like this where almost all of the women were covered. For her, this was completely normal. The fashion show, after all, was targeting Kuwaiti brides. These were the daughters and their female relatives of Kuwaiti families who could afford to buy the dresses that would soon be shown. The audience made perfect sense!

Once the lights went down and the show began, I was in for another big surprise. Instead of seeing the latest modest Islamic fashion trends on the runway, practically naked models appeared one by one. They each strode down the runway in nude-colored evening dresses with sequins strategically placed on their tall slender bodies. These models were from a modeling agency in the United Arab Emirates that employed women from mostly Russia and eastern European countries. They were beautiful, and the seemingly transparent dresses they modeled were dazzling. I just did not expect this sort of dress would be what some Kuwaiti women wanted to wear at their wedding parties.

I should have had an inkling of what women liked to wear at wedding parties when I visited a shoe store just inside the 1,300-foot high Al-Hamra business tower in downtown Kuwait. I was drawn inside by the gorgeous display of sparkling silver shoes in the shop window. The heels were six inches high. There were a couple of women in the store wearing their black *abayyas* busy trying on the shoes. I couldn't help but ask one of them in Arabic if the six-inch heels were comfortable to walk in. She looked at me and said in perfect English, "These shoes are not for walking. They are for dancing!" She explained the shoes were for ladies'-only wedding celebrations. I had not known at the time that such shoes would go perfectly with the sequined evening gowns like the ones I saw on the *Bourgeoisie* runway.

Wearing these sexy dresses and fancy shoes in the privacy of their homes or to women's-only wedding parties was perfectly appropriate. Single women in particular liked such dresses because they want to look as beautiful and as sexy as possible. At every wedding party, potential mothers-in-law are present looking for just the right girls for their sons. If mothers of young beautiful daughters meet mothers of young eligible sons, a match in heaven might be made.

Marriage is serious business in Kuwait, literally. Many marriages -- but not all -- are arranged through parental intervention based on family business interests as well as social appearances. Parents scrutinize potential candidates and their families for possible signs of dishonor that might undermine their social standing in the community. In Kuwait, one way to ensure propriety has been marriage between cousins. Intermarriage not only has kept wealth in the form of a dowry or inheritance within the family, it has helped promise greater loyalty among family members. Historically this has been especially important to the Bedouin tribes living in the Arabian desert where there were no walls to protect them.[lxiii] By intermarrying within their tribe, *'assibiya,* or "group feeling," was reinforced. This strong tribal identification and unity within the tribe helped to defend against the constant threat of raids from other tribes. [lxiv] Daughters could be relied on to care for their young and elderly kin while sons would fight harder to protect them. This strong need to build and maintain this tribal group-feeling remains important even today for Kuwaitis.

Science today has exposed the genetic dangers posed by familial intermarrying, especially between first cousins. Consanguineous marriages, according to scientific research, predispose offspring to serious genetic defects that cause debilitating diseases like Thalassemia.[lxv] Thalassemia is a blood disorder passed down through families in which the body makes an abnormal form of hemoglobin that leads to anemia.[lxvi] The large number of cases in Kuwait has spurred the Kuwaiti Ministry of Health to implement a law requiring pre-marriage medical checks tracing the hereditary history of both the bride and groom's families. The idea is that if the couple, especially those who are first cousins, discovers that they are likely to bring very sick children into the world, they and their families are counseled to break off the marriage. If they go through with the wedding, Kuwaiti authorities will not register their marriages officially. Though this sounds like a pretty serious response, intermarrying sadly continues in Kuwait I am told, but given the lack of official support, it is hoped this tradition will eventually come to an end. Soroptomist International in Kuwait is working to raise awareness about the disease and are raising funds to build a center for people who suffer from blood disorders in Kuwait. They are also lobbying authorities to make it more difficult legally for couples to marry knowing they both are carriers of this extremely painful and life-threatening blood disease.

My husband was invited to dozens of weddings in Kuwait. It was an honor to have distinguished guests like ambassadors visit the male-only wedding parties to congratulate the fathers of the bride and groom as well as the groom himself. He typically attended these wedding parties after work around five or six o'clock in the evening in his business suit. The receptions were a great way for him to show respect to the various Kuwaiti families without having to spend a lot of time. He would spend no more than 15 minutes to greet and congratulate the hosts because that was all that was expected.

The large number of wedding invitations that my husband received was seldom extended to me. Attending a women's wedding party is a whole different story. It isn't possible to go just to greet the mothers of the bride and groom and wish the bride well. Women who attend these parties are expected to stay for several hours and not leave until after a sumptuous banquet is served around midnight. Women prepare for hours to attend these weddings, mostly in salons where they spend enormous amounts of money to do their makeup, hair and nails. False eyelashes and hair extensions are the norm. Then they wear their fancy dresses, often bought from the finest stores in Paris and London, and glamorous shoes, always careful that they are not seen in the same outfit twice. Wedding invitations for women are a huge commitment. Once Kuwaitis began to know me, I received more invitations and when I attended their weddings, I was not home until one o'clock in the morning. I was thankful Kuwaiti women did not expect me to attend all the weddings in town like the men expected from my husband. It would have been impossible for me to keep up, physically and financially.

One day, I received a wedding invitation on my Instagram account. I had developed a public persona by creating an Instagram account, and after a year, I had garnered almost 300 followers which was a lot for me at the time. I did not share photos of my family, but I did post pictures of all the wonderful things I was doing in Kuwait as the wife of the U.S. ambassador. I quickly learned that Instagram was a major way Kuwaitis liked to communicate and share information. Instagram was also a convenient way to meet Kuwaitis, especially Kuwaiti women, and for them to get to know me. I actually had friends whom I considered my "Instagram friends" and when I saw them in town, I always greeted them warmly as if we were long, lost friends. We grew to like each other by what we saw in the photos we chose to post.

When I received the wedding invitation on Instagram, I was at first hesitant because I had only met the woman who invited me briefly at a conference held at Kuwait University. I had no specific recollection of her or the meeting. She sent me access to her Instagram, and so I could learn a little more about her. She was the mother of the bride who had spent several years in the States studying at the University of Southern California. When I had met her, she wore the traditional black *abayya* and *hijab* and that is how she was seen in her Instagram photos. I was intrigued about going and I readily accepted her invitation once I learned it was to be held at the exquisite Jumeirah Hotel, a well-known venue for weddings.

I arrived at 9:00 pm. I could have arrived earlier, but I knew it would be a very late night. Before I entered the wedding hall at the hotel, I was asked to check my cell phone and handed it over to a guard. There were to be no personal photographs because the women attending the wedding did not want their faces to be shown since most of them covered in public. The venue at the hotel was arranged much like the fashion show. Instead of a runway, there was a long dance floor lined by rows of seats for ladies to sit on either side.

I arrived alone and was politely given a seat in the front row, prime real estate at a wedding. At first the rather plump woman I was to sit next to on the narrow couch refused to move over, and I practically fell off the side of the bench. Someone came to my rescue by physically taking the women's hands and lifting her over a few inches. I learned later she had four sons and none of them were yet married. She only spoke Arabic, but I could tell she was an important guest. She had a front row seat to assess the bounty of young girls who would eventually dance across the floor. No one really paid much attention to me or knew me except the mother of the bride who invited me, and she was occupied with her daughter.

No males were allowed in the room. The wait staff and the photographer were all female, mainly from the Philippines. The DJ's voice was male, but he was sitting in another room while a woman with a walkie-talkie gave him instructions. With no men in sight, the invited female guests felt comfortable taking off their veils once they were inside the hotel room. They kept their veils in bags next to their seats, ready for when they needed to cover. The dresses they wore to the party were incredible. Most were very expensive designer dresses. Some dresses exposed cleavage; others had high slits, but I did not see any *La Bourjoisie* dresses that evening. I loved the fact that everyone at the wedding was considered beautiful. It did not matter whether you were thin or fat; tall or short; young or old. Everyone accepted each other as they strutted their stuff down the dance floor in the middle of the room.

The young girls led the dancing up and down the dance floor. They swayed to the beat of Arabic music as they glided forward together across the floor. I joined them a couple of times and from what I could tell, the dance was a slow and steady three-step pattern, like the cha-cha-cha, except with a gentle shaking of hips and shoulders. Dancing in Kuwait is more serene than the more athletic *dabke* folk-dancing of the Levant or the strenuous belly-dancing of Egypt. Eventually, one of the friends of the woman who invited me found a seat next to me. She stayed with me the rest of the evening. She had also studied in the States and became a forensic scientist now working in Kuwait. I enjoyed her company very much, especially since she explained everything that was happening.

The Arabic music and dancing went on until about 11:00 pm. Then the large doors opened and the bride entered the room. She was gorgeous. She was dressed in a traditional white bridal gown. Her mother escorted her down the floor to the stage at the front of the room. It was a beautiful sight. All the ladies, including myself, went up to get a picture with her on an elegant couch placed on the illumined stage before rows of tall flowers. About a half hour later, there was a sudden rush from the ladies returning to their seats. Word was that the groom and his immediate family were arriving any moment. The doors suddenly closed, and everyone put their black *abayyas* back on in preparation. Only a few of us in the room did not cover, including the bride. This was her day to show her beauty before her guests and soon, her husband's family, including only his closest male relatives.

Sometimes when a larger group of males from outside the family come into the wedding hall, the bride will also cover. This happened when one of our more outgoing male embassy officers talked his way into accompanying an extended group of male family and friends to meet the bride at another wedding I went to. Sure enough, the bride covered herself in a white cloak, placing her white hood so that it draped over her face as well. She was awfully nice to accommodate the men's group. A Kuwaiti woman told me she would never allow males outside the immediate family to enter her wedding precisely because she did not want to have to cover on her most special day, nor did she want to have anything mess up her carefully coiffed hair.

Once the ladies were ready, having transformed the room from an array of color to the stern black of their *abayyas*, the groom, his father, and the father of the bride, accompanied by the brothers on both sides walked down the dance floor to join the bride on stage. It was beautiful to see both families unite. The happy mood in the room affirmed that this marriage was based on love and had the potential to last forever. It was after midnight, and I tried to leave but first I was commanded to share in the feast prepared in the large banquet hall of the hotel. Sometime after the wedding I learned via Instagram that the mother of the bride was in the hospital. I had sent a thank you note, and she wrote back saying she was resting there after complaining of being so exhausted she could hardly walk. I could only imagine that the planning that went into her daughter's wedding must have been incredibly stressful.

Wedding traditions have not really changed much in Kuwait. The only changes that have occurred, according to the Kuwaiti forensic scientist I spoke with at the wedding, concern the venue and the music. Today wedding parties have moved from the family home into the big hotels which has become very expensive. A hotel general manager who operates one of the largest wedding halls in town told me that the price tag of one particularly extravagant wedding I would later attend was 70,000 Kuwaiti Dinars, the equivalent of over $230,000![lxvii]

The flower arrangements were out of this world, and there were also two female singers from North Africa. Given the high price of renting hotel space and the lavish dinners being served, families have tried to cut back on costs by hiring DJ's to play Arabic music rather than expensive live performers.

Some Kuwaiti families try to hold weddings outside normal traditions and expectations, but this is very difficult. One Kuwaiti woman confided in me that she was determined to hold her daughter's wedding during the day because she simply did not enjoy eating at 1:00 am. Another said she liked the idea of mixed weddings where men and women celebrate together and that she hoped she could have a wedding like this. Though there may be those who dream of doing things differently, it is unlikely that the essence of Kuwaiti weddings will change. This is one of the signature cultural events of this tiny Gulf country, and as long as people are able, these weddings will continue with the same joy and exuberance, following the same traditions they always have.

Before wedding celebrations like these take place, a contract between the groom and the ranking male member, known in Arabic as the *wakeel*, of the bride's family is signed. According to our U.S. embassy website that provides information to American citizens contemplating marriage to Kuwaitis, either an authorized religious figure or a judge and two male witnesses must be present for the signing of the contract. The bride's representative is normally her father, but a brother, uncle, or even the officiator of the marriage can also serve as her legal representative. The important thing to note here is that women are not directly involved in this contract, despite the fact that it will affect their lives forever. The contract is the domain of male members of the family in Kuwait.

Women have become wiser, however, about the importance of this contract. It is during the wedding contract negotiations that certain expectations can be deliberated and agreed to in the marriage. As in a prenuptial agreement, women can negotiate terms about issues that they know would upset them in the marriage. A Muslim husband's legal ability to have up to four wives at the same time, provided he is able to support them equally is one particularly sensitive issue that can be addressed in the contract. A woman cannot forbid the right of her husband to have four wives in the contract, because this would be tantamount to contradicting Islamic law. But she may -- with permission of the groom and the officiator -- include a clause that her husband must accept her request for a divorce should he take another wife. An American woman who has been married to a Kuwaiti for almost 40 years had this clause written into her wedding contract. Her husband to this day has not taken another wife because he knows he would lose his first.

At an *'aza* or condolence call I made for the passing of a prominent Kuwaiti scientist, I visited a grieving Kuwaiti first wife who did not have such a clause in her wedding contract. She was forced to live the remaining years of her husband's life devastated by his decision to take a second wife. Because the deceased man's second wife was an American physician and was known to the U.S. embassy, it was thought that I should go to condole her. No one at our embassy was aware that there was another wife, a first wife, and mistakenly sent me to her house. After I went through the condolence line of grieving family members, I was asked to sit next to the first wife. Confused, I inquired about the American doctor to whom the embassy thought I should condole.

The first wife looked at me in disbelief and quickly let it be known that she was the *real* wife and that this other woman was not attending the family *'aza* because she was not welcome. Oh, I thought, I really messed this up. The first wife went on to say she had been married to her now dead husband for 23 years before he left the family home to live with his second wife. Her three daughters quickly gathered around and chimed in to support their mother as their father's only true wife. My heart went out to them, not only for the loss of their father, but the emotional stress he had put on all of them during his life. Nonetheless, they were very touched that the wife of the American ambassador had come to grieve with them and graciously welcomed me to stay. In Kuwait, such mix-ups are not uncommon, as the number of wives a man has is not readily advertised. I have to say I had no desire to meet the second wife, certainly not after learning how Kuwaiti women abhor that their husbands have the right to marry up to four wives. Even though the caveat is that each wife must be treated equally, it is almost impossible that this can happen given the complications in dividing property ownership and inheritance. Some believe that having more than one wife should be made illegal precisely because it is impossible to carry out the letter of the law to treat each woman equally in terms of her standing in the family and its possessions.

With all the effort that goes into a Kuwaiti wedding, I was sad to read in a Kuwait Times article that the divorce rate in Kuwait had risen to a whopping 50 percent by 2015.[lxviii] Reasons for the high divorce rate, according to the article, were attributed to the young ages of the brides and grooms, their lack of preparedness, and pressure from their parents to marry people who may not be right for each other. In this modern age where the younger generation has so many more opportunities, couples contemplating marriage need time to consider the consequences of deciding to marry. The more I met Kuwaiti women, the more I saw how strong and independent they were, and how they also had their own hopes, dreams, and ambitions. Hopefully Kuwaiti men will become more willing to accept this in today's Kuwaiti women, and together they find ways to make their marriages last forever. Hopefully they will at least wait until they are older and learn more about each other to ascertain whether they are truly compatible as partners for life.

# CHAPTER EIGHT

## *Ramadan Nights*

I have lived in several Islamic countries, but I have never seen such joy during the month-long fasting period of Ramadan as I witnessed in Kuwait. The joy, of course, is found at night after the end of the fast. For this month, life in the desert is lived as it should be lived, under the cover of night rather than the blazing sun of the day.

Ramadan, in summer 2015, began on June 18 and lasted to July 17 when the *Eid al-Fitr*, the Celebration of Ending the Fast or Sugar Feast, marked its end based on the sighting of the crescent moon. The long summer days in Kuwait that year lasted a full 16 hours. One of our embassy drivers, an Egyptian living in Kuwait, joked he was glad he was not living in Iceland where daylight lasted a full 22 hours! Certainly, I thought, it would be impossible to fast for 22 hours each day. The driver explained that Muslims in Iceland were permitted to fast according to the time zone in Mecca, Saudi Arabia, instead. A *fatwa* was issued to help Muslims fast in places where the sun stays up for so long. Today, Islamic scholars can provide rulings to help Muslims remain faithful no matter where they are or whatever challenge they face in the modern world. These rulings are called *fatwas*. How scholars interpret Islamic law has a huge impact on Islamic society today. The problem has been that interpretations have varied widely, from leading Muslims to progress rationally in modern society to dragging them back to the 7th century.

Ramadan is the ninth month of the Islamic lunar calendar. Fasting during daylight hours during this month is an annual observance by Muslims worldwide and one of the five pillars of Islam. These pillars are the essential tenets of Islam that Muslims are expected to adhere to in order to be considered true followers who submit themselves to the will of God. The other pillars are to recite the declaration of faith that there is only one God, pray five times a day, give alms to the poor, and perform a pilgrimage to Mecca if one can afford it. Regarding the first pillar, I once asked a Jesuit Catholic priest from Malta I knew in Turkey if Muslims and Christians pray to the same God. He surprised me when he said no. In his view, the God of Islam is strict and judgmental, while God in Christianity is loving and forgiving.[lxix] I had always thought there was only one God as in the Muslim concept of *ahl al-kitab*, "people of the book," inferring that the world's great monotheistic religions shared a common deity. Unfortunately, I learned that religion is more complicated and less unifying than I had originally thought.

During the fast of the holy month of Ramadan, the fourth pillar of Islam, Muslims should not eat, drink, or smoke between sunrise and sunset. The purpose of fasting is to experience hunger and deprivation and to demonstrate self-discipline, humility, and faith.[lxx] Clearly, this is not easy, and it is a badge of honor for those who are able to make it through. One day during lunch with a western ambassador's wife at my home, she raised an uncomfortable possibility, suggesting that Kuwaitis were eating in the privacy of their homes during the day instead of actually fasting. She was very skeptical that people could go the entire day without eating. After all, what goes on in the privacy of home is different than what goes on in public. Why not eat during the day in private and then go out in the evenings to celebrate? I found myself resisting this view. Thinking back on my own experiences living in Islamic countries, I remember meeting many Muslims who fasted. Muslims take great pride in their discipline and faith in fasting. This is not to say that all Muslims fast during Ramadan. As *Desert Girl* noted on her online blog about Ramadan in Kuwait, "you can always tell a Kuwaiti who does not fast because he is standing in front of the take-away counter at the Sultan Center grocery store at noon."[lxxi] It is really no big deal. For me, the important thing is to respect those who are fasting by not eating, drinking, or smoking in front of them, and not judge those who are not.

Although I truly enjoyed Kuwaiti nightlife during Ramadan, I have to admit I found getting through the day challenging. I had heard Ramadan was very strict in the Gulf, but I had no idea the same restrictions would apply to non-Muslims as well. I recalled during my last post in Ankara, Turkey, that there were plenty of restaurants open during Ramadan in the day to eat and drink. Not in Kuwait. All the restaurants were shut down during daylight hours. In Kuwait, eating, drinking (even water), and smoking in public places were strictly prohibited to both Muslims and non-Muslims. Kuwaiti authorities could fine people caught eating or drinking in public, and the police had the authority to imprison anyone violating these prohibitions during Ramadan.[lxxii]

For me, it was not being able to drink water in public that bothered me most. Over the years, I came to equate drinking lots of water with good health. This seemed to be especially important since I was living in the desert in over 110-degree heat. I was genuinely surprised to discover that my health club also did not allow the public consumption of water during Ramadan. Warning notices were posted around the gym, reminding members to respect Kuwaiti Ramadan laws, including no drinking water in public. Having my health club tell me I could not drink water seemed outrageous. The whole Ramadan atmosphere in Kuwait at first seemed extreme, almost threatening, but eventually, I got over it. I exercised without water and learned my body could adjust. I let my whole life turn upside down after the first week of Ramadan. I was sleeping late into the morning, because I was always out past midnight. I was skipping breakfast to allow room for a midnight meal. I was way off my routine and, somehow, felt strangely content living in this new and happy universe.

In Kuwait, Ramadan after sunset is a time to host family and friends to break the fast with the *iftar* meal served at sunset. I generally did not attend these *iftar* meals. For one thing, it was best not to be on the roads before sunset because this was when the big rush to get home occurred. It was dangerous to be on the roads with speeding cars filled with hungry people trying to get home before the sun went down. This is true in all the Muslim countries during Ramadan that I have lived in.

What I did do was attend the ladies *diwaniyyas* held after the *iftar* meals in the evenings, especially during the first week. By the second week, I started receiving invitations to the late-night meals known as *gubkas* hosted during Ramadan, and served around midnight. Each time I visited a Kuwaiti home during Ramadan, I was greeted cheerfully with, *"Ramadan Karim! Mubarak Alykum Al-shahar! Asahik min 'Awadah!"* Happy Ramadan! Have a Blessed Month! Many Returns! Once I memorized these important Arabic phrases, I partook in their greetings and well-wishes which were well received and appreciated.

I also bought a couple of traditional *dera'a* kaftans -- the colorful long dresses adorned with intricate embroidery and glittering details -- and wore them to celebrate with the other women. These dresses are easy to find in Kuwait, and they also make for successful home businesses. There are many Kuwaiti designers who make their own dresses and sell them at the various crafts markets held around town. These *dera'a* can be very expensive. I bought mine at an exclusive secondhand shop where Kuwaiti women donated their seasonal Ramadan attire for charity, never expecting to wear the same thing again anyway.

Designing for Muslim women in general has become more and more popular. I recently read in the Kuwait Times that *Dolce and Gabbana*, the Italian fashion gurus known for their sultry look, have created a new collection of *abayya* and *hijab* for the Gulf market. Their motto, according to the article, is *"dressing modestly does not have to mean dressing drab."*[lxxiii] Their new line consists of dark shaded ankle-length dresses with bright motifs. D&G sunglasses, designer bags, and oversized jewelry help complete the look. Not wanting to miss out on this lucrative luxury market, other top designer brands have also introduced collections for the Muslim women's market, including Oscar de la Renta, DKNY, and Tommy Hilfiger. These new styles are really quite beautiful and the fashion trend is spreading fast.[lxxiv]

One evening, I had the honor to attend the *diwaniyya* of Shaykha Alanoud Ahmed Jaber al-Sabah, the sister of the Amir of Kuwait, who lives in a lovely palace. As the embassy driver dropped me under the awesome grand entryway, I couldn't help but notice the other cars rolling up behind us. There were plenty of Bentleys, Benzes, and BMW's and other fancy cars. Upon entering the palace through a main hall, I walked into a central salon with a soaring ceiling. Colorful couches with satin pillows provided comfortable seating and enhanced the exquisite oriental setting. Ladies in their lavishly decorated kaftans sat together, and the room was filled with conversation. The Sheikha holds her *diwaniyya* for three consecutive nights at the beginning of each Ramadan. This was the third night and there was still magic in the air.

Watching Kuwaiti mothers and their daughters stream into the living room dressed in their very best to greet the Amir's sister was a feast to my eyes. At one point, a large group of men also entered the room dressed in their long white *dishdashas* and *gutras* (headgear), covered with their gold trimmed black *bishts* (cloaks) to pay their respect to the Sheikha as well. The men were family members of the Al-Sabah. As the Al-Sabah family tends to be progressive in their outlook, I did not see any of the women take cover under *abayyas*. Sheikha

Alanoud, meanwhile, well into her seventies if not older, was warm and energetic. She made sure I was comfortable by looking my way from time to time with a big smile.

A few days later, she sent over her finest Ramadan cooking to our residence at the embassy. The meal arrived in eight large beautiful copper dishes covered with Moroccan-style tajine tops. We were surprised to receive such a feast and were truly overwhelmed by her generosity. Kuwaiti cuisine is delicious in the way it infuses Persian and Indian spices into Arabian and Mediterranean dishes. Each covered pot was filled with a special Kuwaiti dish, including a couple of fresh herbal salads, *machboos* made of lamb and pungent rice, chicken and rice *biryani*, curry, ochre, and flatbread. The Sheikha also included her own celebrated Ramadan dessert known as *sub al-gafshas*, which resemble small fried doughnut holes, but are spiced and fragrant. I wondered how our small family could possibly eat it all. We decided to share it with Doug's bodyguards from the Kuwait National Guards. We learned later it was customary for Kuwaiti families to provide food to their neighbors and friends, as well as to the poor during Ramadan. The tradition was also to return the pots as soon as they were no longer needed, and so we made sure to do just that.

I was also invited, along with the other wives of ambassadors assigned to Kuwait, to attend the women's *diwaniyya* held at the palace of Sheikha Sharifa bint Sulaiman Al-Jasem, wife of Crown Prince Sheikh Nawaf Al-Ahmad Al-Jaber Al-Sabah. An Amiri Decree on February 7, 2006, officially designated her husband as the Crown Prince of Kuwait. If anything were to happen to the current Amir, the country would embrace her husband as the next Amir. His elevation to the position of Amir, however, would leave open the position of Crown Prince. Although Kuwait's succession is not put to a general election, it is subject to a legislative vote when it comes to choosing the Crown Prince.[lxxv] Needless to say, political jockeying for this important position has already begun.

Thus, Sheikha Sharifa may one day be Kuwait's First Lady, a position that has not been filled in Kuwait for a very long time. The current Amir, Sabah Al-Sabah, has been widowed since 1990. It would be interesting to see what a Kuwaiti First Lady would do in her role. For the time being, however, this lovely woman and mother of four sons and a daughter is now a cancer survivor. In fact, during her *diwaniyya*, she was still recuperating from her cancer treatments. She seemed quite tired and frail. Everyone appreciated her strength in deciding to hold her Ramadan event in her home so soon after her recovery. She was really very kind to have invited the diplomatic corps spouses to her salon. Her guest hall was magnificent, with a huge array of beautiful orchids dominating the center of the room. Her family and friends did their best to make us feel welcome, and it was a true honor to be there.

Doug and I also attended a couple of mixed *diwaniyyas* together. One was held by Sheikha Rasha al-Sabah. She was a former minister and senior advisor to the Amir. Her sister Scheherazade told us that Rasha had been a brilliant child growing up and that she received her Ph.D. from Yale University. There was something very energetic in Sheikha Rasha's demeanor, despite her recent cancer treatment in New York City. She was not your typical Kuwaiti woman, since she wore pants and had a close-cropped hairstyle. These Ramadan evenings were certainly introducing me to some truly fascinating Kuwaitis.

While I received several invitations to ladies' *diwaniyyas*, my schedule paled in comparison to my husband's. As far as I could tell, he was going through herculean efforts to attend as many men's *diwaniyyas* as was physically possible. As in weddings, men are not expected to stay more than 10 minutes. One night, he managed to go to 14 separate *diwaniyyas* with the help of his driver and security guards who mapped out an intricate route to accomplish this goal. It became a bit of competition with the other diplomats in town to see how many *diwaniyyas* they could attend in a single night. Having a large Surburban vehicle fitted with lights, siren, and megaphone to protect the black Cadillac Doug rode in, gave my husband an enormous advantage over the other ambassadors who did not travel with the same level of security.

In all, Doug managed to attend a total of 64 different family *diwaniyyas* in the eight days of Ramadan that passed before everything shut down when a bomb went off at the Imam As-Sadiq Mosque downtown on June 26, 2015. It's hard to believe we really only had eight nights of experiencing the joy of Ramadan before the bombing. The tone of Ramadan changed immediately after that bombing. Our Ramadan nights had been cut short. The evening gatherings and late night dinners were immediately cancelled as the country dove into mourning for the lives lost from this devastating terrorist attack.

Although the Ramadan nights of 2015 never returned to the same level of enthusiasm as before the bombing, a week later, the children's Ramadan tradition known as the *Gerge'an* resumed according to schedule. This festive tradition typically is held on the 13th, 14th and 15th day of Ramadan. The origins of the word *Gerge'an* comes from the Kuwaiti Arabic word, "*garga'a*", referring to the noisy sound of the old iron cans that were once filled with sweets. The idea of giving the children sweets was to help them through their fasting and to reward them for their efforts. After the *iftar* meals, children dressed in traditional costumes and went into their neighborhoods, knocking on doors to sing traditional Kuwaiti songs. The children would hold bags in the hope of receiving candy and nuts in return. Some like to compare this tradition to Halloween but without the scary goblins and witches.

Today *Gerge'ans* have become somewhat commercialized as many corporations now sponsor events for the children. Parents are less likely now to allow their children to go out on the streets to sing anyway because there are so many cars and careless drivers. It is more common instead to have corporations invite children to their headquarters and entertain them with shows and games, promoting at the same time their company's goodwill. Our own U.S. embassy held a *gerge'an* for our local employees and their families. It was really fun and included lots of games, music, and children dancing, in addition to plenty of sweets for the kids. I was also invited to attend a wonderful *gerge'an* held by the Kuwaiti Society for the Guardians of the Disabled. It was a nice opportunity for the children in their care to celebrate the holy month of Ramadan together. *Gerge'ans* are strictly a Kuwaiti tradition though other countries have begun to adopt the custom. It does not surprise me that Kuwaitis would conceive of such a happy custom during Ramadan. It fits with their warm hearts and love for their children.

# CHAPTER NINE

## *Imbalance in the Law*

Like all societies and nations, Kuwait was not without divisive politics. A small country, the issues bubbling under the surface were easy to spot living as an outsider. As the wife of an ambassador, I was welcomed just about everywhere, and so I sometimes felt as though I had a bird's eye view of the country since I was able to move through many social circles. The one topic I heard most often discussed by women was the country's legal system. Many Kuwaiti laws are embedded in Kuwait's Personal Status Laws which are derived from Islamic law and do not treat men and women equally. In fact, some of these Personal Status Laws run counter to Kuwait's own constitution. Article 29 of the Kuwaiti Constitution, for example, states *"all people are equal in human dignity and in public rights and duties before the law, without distinction to race, origin, language, or religion."*[lxxvi] Assuming women are included in "all people", it would seem then that some of these Personal Status Laws upheld in Kuwaiti courts are in direct conflict with the Constitution.

These Personal Status Laws concerning inheritance and divorce are steeped in history and culture and often take precedence over civilian law. In the Gulf, for instance, the treatment of women as a man's property has a long history and even continued openly well into the 20th century.[lxxvii] An Al-Sabah family member once told my husband that princes and tribal rulers in the Gulf in the first half of the 20th century regularly presented prominent guests with concubines or slaves, in the same way modern Gulf rulers bestow cars, Arabian horses, and extravagant watches today. In Kuwait, he added, men from prominent families and wealthy merchants often took concubines in addition to being married to four wives in those years. In this way, they could have more women in their domain without offending their religion.

He mentioned one prominent Kuwaiti family of more than ten brothers and sisters. Several were born of the father's first wife. However, quite a few were born to the father's concubine as well. A Kuwaiti businessman who knew this particular family well explained that the concubine was brought to Kuwait from Africa at the age of seven as a servant of the first wife. As the servant matured, she became the husband's concubine. When asked if the man could marry a concubine who gave birth to his own children, he responded that it was possible if he first "released her from service." In this particular instance, the man did release his concubine from service and married her for love.

There are plenty of reminders of slavery's former prominence in Kuwaiti society. At a late-night Ramadan *ghabka* during my second year in Kuwait, I was invited to the home of a family who gathered all the descendants their beloved deceased father's four wives and concubines to celebrate. The woman who invited me was very open about her father's array of love interests. While she was very matter of fact, my prudish American upbringing made me rather uncomfortable. There must have been 100 women who arrived to the *ghabka* that night, many of them somehow connected to this man whose portrait loomed large on the main wall beaming down on all those assembled in the family's ornate living room. Her father was a prominent landowner who died in the 1960's, leaving behind enormous wealth for his many children descended from his four wives and the concubines who came into the family by way of the trade routes to Africa. This man, however, did not live to see the change brought by the ruling family under Amir Sheikh 'Abdallah Salem al-Sabah who abolished the practice of slavery in Kuwait in 1963. In that year the Amir signed the United Nations convention advocating an end to all forms of slavery with the intention of modernizing his country and elevating the treatment of women.

Not all discrimination against women in Kuwaiti law, however, has its roots in traditional Arab Gulf culture. As colonizers of the Middle East in the 19th century, both Britain and France introduced legal systems into the region at a time when British and French cultures were distinctly discriminatory toward women. The most egregious laws in the Arab world concern honor killing which provide leniency to men who kill their female relatives accused of adultery. These laws were in fact introduced in Kuwaiti law through the French Napoleonic Penal Code.[lxxviii] French civil code had a significant influence in the Middle East once Egyptian scholars translated it into Arabic, and it was adopted into Egyptian Civil Code. Because it was already translated into Arabic and established in Egypt, it was attractive to other newly established Arab nations at the time. Kuwait, for example, when it became independent in 1961, decided to make Egyptian Civil Code and *Shari'a* law the cornerstones of its legal system. Thus, the legal cover found in Kuwaiti law today enabling a man to commit violence against a woman due to her infidelity was originally derived from French civil law.[lxxix]

In the 1810 French Penal Code, Article 324, Title II, Chapter 1, Section 1 specifically states: *"Murder, committed by the husband, upon his wife, or by the wife, upon her husband, is not excusable, if the life of the husband or wife, who has committed such murder, has not been put in peril, at the very moment when the murder has taken place. Nevertheless, in the case of adultery... murder committed upon the wife as well as upon her accomplice, at the moment when the husband shall have caught them in the fact, in the house where the husband and wife dwell, is excusable."*

England also promulgated law in the 19th century that was similarly discriminatory against women. The country's *1857 Divorce and Matrimonial Causes Act* allowed men to divorce their wives on the simple grounds of her adultery, while a woman had to prove her act of adultery was caused by desertion, or by cruelty, rape, sodomy, incest or bigamy. This was the law in Britain until 1923, when the grounds of divorce were made the same for both sexes.[lxxx] So while Europe has since rewritten its 200-year old laws that deprived women of equal rights, Kuwait as well as many Muslim and Arab countries have not yet come around.

Experts estimate that somewhere between 5,000 and 20,000 honor killings occur per year worldwide.[lxxxi] Most also agree that the preponderance of honor killings occur in Muslim countries or in expatriate Muslim communities.[lxxxii] A 2013 Pew Research Center Poll found that majorities in Pakistan, Bangladesh, Afghanistan, Jordan, Iraq, Egypt, the Palestinian territories, and Tajikistan believed killing a woman over honor was at least sometimes justified.[lxxxiii] In Jordan, most shockingly, 81% said a man should never be killed over honor, but only 34% said the same of killing a woman.[lxxxiv]

Honor killing remains a glaring legal injustice. It has largely been accepted in patriarchal Arab society because men are seen as having the right to defend their families' honor and therefore, to exact their own punishment in matters of *zinna* (illicit sex). Many women have been killed simply because a male relative suspected them of contemplating an improper act even if it was only a matter of being seen alone with a man. While honor killing is not very common among Kuwaitis, there have been sporadic incidents mainly involving Syrian and Jordanian expatriate families living in Kuwait.

One incident, however, involved a Kuwaiti in an honor killing in Dorset, Great Britain, in October 2014. According to the British newspaper *Daily Mail,* a 59-year old Kuwaiti man stabbed his 24-year old daughter in the neck 13 times in their apartment where he was chaperoning her while she studied English. After being taken to the hospital for his own self-inflicted wounds after the murder, the father asked the surgeon what the penalties for honor killings were in Britain. The father explained he had done what he did because his daughter had dishonored him by talking on the phone and asking him to leave the apartment. "It's all about the honor," he said.[lxxxv] Although British authorities later diagnosed him with serious psychological problems, it is quite possible the Kuwaiti may have rationalized his country's leniency toward killing in the name of honor as a right to kill his own daughter. This is the danger of having such a law on the books.

Honor killing has deep historic roots long before Islam and western civilization came into existence. In the book "Half the Sky," by Nicholas D. Kristof and Sheryl WuDunn, the authors researched the tradition of killing girls suspected of losing their virginity out of wedlock and discovered how widespread the practice was around the world. "The cult of virginity," as they called it, was even found in the Bible. The authors cited a passage from the Old Testament of the Hebrews in Deuteronomy 22:13: "*If a man takes a wife and, after lying with her, dislikes her and slanders her and gives her a bad name, saying, 'I married this woman, but when I approached her, I did not find proof of her virginity,' then the girl's father and mother...shall display the cloth (that the couple slept on) before the elders of the town....If, however, the charge is true and no proof of the girl's virginity can be found, she shall be brought to the door of her father's house and there the men of her town shall stone her to death.*"[lxxxvi]

Kristof and WuDunn provided other examples of the ancient complicity in committing violence against women suspected of adultery. They mentioned the ancient Athenian lawgiver, Solon, "*who prescribed that no Athenian could be sold into slavery save a woman who lost her virginity before marriage.*" And they cited a neo-Confucian from the Song Dynasty in China stating, "*For a woman to starve to death is a small matter, but for her to lose her chastity is a calamity.*"[lxxxvii]

Civil society has worked hard to change this attitude toward women in many regions of the world, but having an authoritative figure challenge it directly is probably the most effective solution. In the West, where Christianity was early embraced, it took Jesus to challenge violence against women when he preached one day against the stoning of a woman caught in adultery. In the Book of John, Chapter 8, Verse 7, he said, *"He that is without sin among you, let him first cast a stone at her."* With these words, Jesus repudiated this shameful practice. Similar authentic rejection of honor killing laws needs to happen in Islamic countries. Women across the Arab world are saying they want this practice publicly and institutionally repudiated.

In the 7th century, the rise of Islam with its introduction of *Shari'a* law addressing rules on marriage and divorce, actually did a lot to improve the status of women by reforming Arabian customary law that treated women as objects. According to N.J. Coulson in his book, *"A History of Islamic Law,"* there were two essential improvements for women that came with the advent of Islam. The first raised the wife from being merely an object for sale to being the subject of "a contracting party who, in return for her granting the right of sexual union with herself, is entitled to receive the due consideration of the dower," the husband's estate.[lxxxviii] For the first time, the wife had a legal standing in the family for inheritance. The second improvement concerned divorce. Prior to Islam, a husband could discard his wife at a moment's notice since her standing was that of a purchased object. The *Qur'an* suspended this right and established instead a waiting period during which time it would be evident whether or not the wife was pregnant. The point was to allow time to enable reconciliation between the couple, but also to ensure financial support should the woman be pregnant.[lxxxix]

Qur'anic law, however, was not intended to restructure tribal society in Arabian culture. It would have been impossible to dismantle the basic social structure centered on the male patriarch. Having written his book in the 1960's, N.J. Coulson cautioned, *"This patriarchal scheme of society is now subjected to the tempering influence of the ethical standard of fair treatment for women."*[xc] It has been 50 years since he wrote his book but it now appears Muslim scholars and politicians, men and women alike, have finally begun to take a closer look at Personal Status Laws and how practically they can address women in modern society. There is growing concern how these laws in particular can continue protecting the Gulf's patriarchal and tribal societies if they do not recognize men and women equally.

There are those in Kuwait, men and women, however, who may not be so interested in achieving real equality in the law. According to Alessandra L. Gonzalez in her book, *"Islamic Feminism in Kuwait,"* many women in Kuwait support the Islamist conservative agenda and are comfortable with the Islamic laws that govern their status. They like the conservative agenda because it focuses on the family. It is less concerned about changing laws and prefers instead to focus on practical issues like longer maternity breaks, shortened workdays, and early retirement packages for career women.[xci] These efforts, as far as they are concerned, enable women to focus on their families and have careers, too. Western women would be in awe, as I was, to see how good Kuwaiti women have it despite imbalance in the law. I recall a Kuwaiti woman I knew, who had a responsible job in one of the government ministries, come into the coffee shop where I happened to be at 3:00 pm. I asked how her day was going, and she said, "great". She was already off from work and ready to attend to herself and her family. Nice, I thought to myself.

It is not surprising then that the Islamist movement in Kuwait has been well supported. Islamist politicians have succeeded in attracting many activists, men and women alike, who meet regularly around town. They are happy to provide emotional and practical support to ordinary people to help them lead productive lives within the Islamic community of laws. When it comes time for elections, these activists are not shy about asking for their votes. Their deep ties in the community have enabled them to secure a significant presence in Parliament.

Many of their supporters are women, and they do not want to jeopardize what they have already achieved. They are less motivated to challenge the conservative family laws that govern their lives. Kuwaiti women, especially the ones I saw covered from head to toe in their black *abayya* and *hijab* in the shopping malls and elsewhere in public, were not necessarily looking to have rights that might undermine their traditions or challenge their religion. On the contrary, they preferred to pursue an Islamic feminist agenda that advanced women's rights in a way that enabled them to remain part of the Islamic community and within Islamic authority.[xcii]

At a conference entitled *"The Role of Contemporary Women in Islamic Societies"* held on February 1, 2016, at Kuwait's National Library, I witnessed Islamic feminists in action. The speakers came from Saudi Arabia, Kuwait, Sudan, Oman, Indonesia, Pakistan, and Bahrain. They were smart, well-educated women, and they were on a mission. They were true to their religion, but they were also seeking a greater stake in the leadership of their countries by participating in the legislative process as well as being activists in their societies.

They each addressed their concerns about the future, especially about their roles as Muslim women in their Muslim-majority countries. The presenter from Indonesia, Zannuba Rahman Wahid, daughter of former Indonesian President Abdurrahman ad-Dakhil who served from 1999 to 2001, however, stood out. Unlike the others, she made an eloquent plea for a review of religious laws within the context of modern society. She went so far as to suggest that younger generations would leave Islam if this was not done.[xciii] She was passionate about Islam and believed it held the solutions to modern-day and called into question some of the longstanding personal status laws.

A Harvard graduate, popularly known as Yenny Wahid, she ruefully ended her talk with a joke about the Muslim family law that allows men to have four wives. The essence of the joke goes something like this: A husband was feeling very ill and his wife was at his side to provide comfort. He wanted to tell the truth about his life in case he died. He cautiously asked his wife, *'Do you know our neighbor?* (pause) *Well, she is actually also my wife.'* His wife gently patted his forehead and patiently responded, *'No worries dear. I understand.'* Feeling relieved, he went on to inform her that his longtime business partner was also his wife. Again, his wife told him not to worry and assured him everything would be okay. He then felt brave enough to tell her that he also had a fourth wife. The wife responded, *'It is all right. Now lie still my dear. Let the poison take its course.'*

With such impressive and strong-willed women leading in the Islamic world, change is going to happen, including in Kuwait. It is just going to look very different from our own feminist revolution. There will be no bras burned in the street or demands for individual freedom over their own bodies. Just as Gloria Steinem and other leaders of the American women's liberation movement, Islamic feminists are going to change the rules of society. The difference will be that Islamic feminists will seek to create a better world through their religion, a world in which the family is sacrosanct. The family is, after all, where women in this part of the world hold their greatest sway. It will be interesting to see how far women will go in terms of challenging men for a greater role in the public domain, beyond issues concerning the family. According to Gonzalez, many Islamist women ultimately support their husbands when it comes to elections and politics. This is why liberal Kuwaitis fear having more women involved in politics, because, ironically, women also could in the end push the country into being even more conservative.[xciv]

# CHAPTER TEN

## *Challenging the Discourse*

There is in Kuwait a band of liberal and progressive women who believe the time has come for their country to provide greater balance and equality in the law. They strive to challenge the strong current of Islamic conservatism in their country. For example, a small group of them has been working steadily for the past few years to abolish Article 153. Article 153 in the Kuwaiti penal code states that any man who surprises his mother, sister, daughter or wife in an unsavory sexual act (*zinna*) with a man and kills her or him or both will be treated as committing a misdemeanor punishable by a maximum of three years jail time and/or a fine of 3,000 rupees (KD 225 or almost $736.00).[xcv] For these women, abolishing Article 153 would be a critical and symbolic move by the government to end a man's legal right to exact justice on the basis of family honor. The fact that this law exists has become a rallying point for these Kuwaiti women who view it as blatant discrimination against women.

As one Kuwaiti activist put it, this law was not about tribal honor at all. In her view, it was really all about a man's *ego* and it had no place in Kuwait's legal framework. During a lunch we held at our residence in January 2016, these activists came to discuss their effort to abolish Article 153. They called their campaign, not surprisingly, "Abolish 153." As a starting point, the women told us how they asked Islamic scholars to review the law to see if it was in accordance with the *Qur'an.* The scholars, well respected in Kuwait, had already informed the group that they could not justify Article 153 as Islamic because the act of honor killing is not specifically addressed in the *Qur'an* or in other authentic Islamic sources. To confirm this, I later asked the lawyer I had met at the Secretariat of Women's Work -- the charitable society connected with Kuwait's Muslim Brotherhood -- about how she viewed efforts to abolish Article 153. She said she was aware of the efforts and found no reason to interfere. So if this law could not be upheld as based in religion, then why was it in existence in the first place?

This group of activists explained some of the concerns they had heard about repealing Article 153 in the National Assembly in Kuwait. Some parliamentarians, they said, were still clinging to their patriarchal ways. These conservative legislators feared repealing the law would only trigger a series of changes they ostensibly perceived to be against Islam, but also a challenge to their own authority. Would the next thing be to make alcohol permissible? Would they be asked to allow sex outside of marriage?[xcvi] It has not been an easy road for the Abolish 153 women who early on suffered the indignity of being taunted as "the *zinna* girls", girls who support illicit sex. These women have not been deterred, however, and I can see from following them on Instagram @abolish153, they have been making progress. They have succeeded in spreading awareness of their efforts and are appealing to their population that Article 153 is senseless.

Having more elected female members serving in the National Assembly would certainly muster support to end this law. For the past couple of years, at least during our tenure in Kuwait from 2014 to 2016, there were no women serving in the legislative body.[xcvii] Women received the right to vote in 2005, but few have been elected. Some say the reason has been that Kuwaiti women voters have been more inclined to support Islamist oriented candidates. In the November 2016 elections, 15 women ran for 50 open seats in Kuwait's 65-member parliament, but only one won: Safa Al Hashem, whose reelection made her the only woman in the legislative body.

When there were women in the parliament, there has been some progress in addressing Kuwait's unequal laws. In October 2009, for example, Kuwaiti courts granted women the right to obtain passports without their husbands' prior consent. The story goes that a complaint was filed by Fatima al-Baghli, a Kuwaiti woman who petitioned the court for the right to obtain a passport without her husband's consent. She had been unable to travel with her children, because her husband was refusing to provide his consent so she could obtain her official documents. It quickly became apparent that thousands of women were also seeking the right to get their passports to travel outside the country, and they also began to petition the courts as well.[xcviii]

The National Assembly in 2009, as this all was unfolding, happened to have four female members. These women were essential to the eventual success of overturning the law preventing women from traveling without their husband's permission. Aseel Al-Awadhi, one of the four female members, enthusiastically cast her vote saying it *"put an end to this injustice against Kuwaiti women."*[xcix] From the beginning, Islamists in the parliament did not make it easy for Ms. Al-Awadhi. Early in her tenure, she had to win the Constitutional Court's favor to allow her to enter the National Assembly without wearing the hijab. Her Islamist colleagues, at the time, did not want her participating in parliament without it. She had already proved herself a fighter.

Changing legislation like the passport law was no small feat, and female parliamentarians were instrumental in making this happen. Having more women in parliament would appear essential in addressing other laws related to marriage, divorce and inheritance, but it is difficult to know, as I mentioned earlier, whether women elected in the future would actually want to support gender equality issues.

Another challenge in trying to change these personal status laws related to marriage, divorce and inheritance laws is the fact that they are derived from *Shari'a* law, and by extension, are drawn from divine authority. But this should not be an excuse for Kuwaiti civil society to give up. Violence against women and domestic abuse, for instance, need to be addressed in terms of how they are dealt with in the law. Unfortunately, these types of issues have been shrouded in secrecy because they could lead to family dishonor. As a result, there are few statistics available to make any conclusions about how widespread violence is in the country. A female physician attending an Abolish 153 meeting held in the spring of 2015 made it clear, however, that domestic abuse is an unspoken problem in Kuwait. She routinely saw battered women come to the emergency room at the hospital where she worked. The police were always called in, but they rarely reported the incidents as domestic abuse. It was just too shameful to the families involved.

I understand from the community of American wives married to Kuwaitis, physical and psychological abuse is especially flagrant when husbands decide to take another wife. Even if the husband is not physically abusive, the emotional insecurity felt by the first wife, who now must compete with another woman with similar legal status in the family, is daunting. I have yet to meet a woman who is not angered by her husband taking another wife. A consular officer from the U.S. embassy once told me after dealing with a difficult domestic violence case involving an American that a Kuwaiti official tried to explain things to her with a very dark joke, *"Once there was a Kuwaiti husband beating his wife in the street. A man came and tried to stop it. The beating continued. Another man came along and again pleaded with the husband to stop. Then the husband asked his wife, do you want me to take a second wife then? And the wife responded, 'Please beat me!'"*

Organizations like Soroptimists International (SI), which established a chapter in Kuwait in October 2015, have put violence against women and gender equality on top of their agenda. The fact that the Kuwaiti government officially recognized this organization is evidence that it understands the need to address women's issues that have been for so long neglected because of the shame they bring. Dr. Stacey Al-Ghawas, who brought SI to Kuwait, hopes to work with other organizations to establish halfway houses for battered women and a hotline for those in crisis. Such work will be challenging since the culture will find it very hard to access lifelines outside their immediate families. The pressure to maintain family honor and not let others know about anything potentially harmful to a family's reputation remains paramount. As in the United States, raising social awareness takes time. You only need to think back to the 1957 movie *"Peyton Place"* and realize how societal constraints concerning honor leave violence unchecked. This movie does a great job of depicting small town America where everyone guards their secrets and social status to the detriment of an abused young woman who was assaulted by her stepfather.

Another issue that has become a rallying point for women is the Personal Status Law that does not allow Kuwaiti women who marry foreign husbands the right to convey their Kuwaiti citizenship to their foreign husbands and their offspring. Hundreds of children are born to Kuwaiti mothers every year who do not have the right to live in Kuwait as full citizens. Consequently, they do not have access to all the social benefits provided to Kuwaiti citizens. What irks so many of these Kuwaiti wives and mothers married to foreigners is the fact that Kuwaiti men, with foreign wives and children, may pass on their citizenship. Meanwhile, the foreign husbands and children of Kuwaiti wives and mothers must apply for residency permits just to remain together as a family and live in Kuwait. According to a leading Kuwaiti scholar and researcher, Dr. AlAnoud Al-Sharekh from Kuwait University's Women's Research and Studies Center, there were 1,704 children born in

2014 alone to Kuwaiti women married to non-nationals. This statistic, according to Dr. Al-Sharekh, who is also a social activist involved in the Abolish 153 Campaign, underscores the need for the Kuwaiti government to reevaluate legislation that governs the lives of these children.[c]

In April 2016, I attended a workshop that was part of Kuwait University's annual Women's Health conference. During an exercise I met by chance a Kuwaiti widow of a foreign marriage. This particular workshop was entitled "*We Are Strong*" and was led by female Kuwaiti Olympic athlete, Balsam Al-Ayub. The goal of the workshop was to encourage women to take initiative whenever they encountered obstacles. "Never change your dream," Balsam said, "change the way **to** your dream. Identify the problem and find a solution. Never be passive!" Her colleague encouraged participants not to feel they must always do what their parents expected if it did not make them happy. Pursuing a career that did not make you happy, she advised, could lead to greater unhappiness later in life. She asked the workshop participants to think about where they wanted to be in five or ten years and advised them to strategize about how they could obtain their goals. She also asked them to think about marrying someone they loved versus someone chosen for them, suggesting that having a true partner in life was more important. The workshop was clearly designed to empower the women in attendance.

Following the presentation, we broke into small groups to work on a problem and come up with solutions to resolve it. I was sitting next to my American friend married to a Kuwaiti when a shy woman dressed in black with a *niqab* covering her face chose to join us to make a group. We were probably less threatening than the group of coquettes next to us with their cute faces showing in their fashionable and colorful modest attire. As the woman approached us, my friend and I could only see her eyes through her glasses peering through the layers of black she wore. As soon as she sat next to us, she poured her heart about her personal problems and wanted us to help.

Breathless, she apologized for wearing the *niqab*, explaining she was mourning the death of her husband several months ago. She was concerned what people would think if she did not cover. The last thing she wanted was for people to think she was looking for another husband so soon. Her problem for our group to address was about how she could obtain a government house now that her husband had passed away. She could no longer afford paying the rent on her current apartment on her government salary. As a widow, the young Kuwaiti woman wanted to move into a government home with her children as soon as possible. In Kuwait's social welfare society, such free assistance to widows can be expected but not always guaranteed. There is often a long list of applicants and not enough housing immediately available. Her saga encapsulated the massive pressures on Kuwait's welfare system.

Making matters worse, the woman revealed that she had been married to an Egyptian, a foreigner, who was not recognized as a Kuwaiti citizen. As a foreigner, he could not own a house in Kuwait but, as the husband, he was still expected to provide for his wife and family, and so he had rented the apartment she was now residing in with their children. If her husband had been Kuwaiti, he would have been eligible to receive upon marriage either a plot of land and a loan to build a house, or a government house.[ci] People sometimes have to wait years to receive these benefits but eventually, if their names are on the list, the government is bound to provide a home for newly married Kuwaiti men. The Egyptian husband, however, was never in line to receive such a house. Even though he had married a Kuwaiti woman, he was prohibited from receiving her citizenship though his livelihood was in Kuwait. The children they brought into the world were also not given full Kuwaiti citizenship and will grow up in Kuwait carrying the passport of their father.

Our distraught friend, however, was determined to receive a government house as a Kuwaiti widow. She had put her name on a list to receive special government housing for widows, but felt that no one from the government was taking her urgency seriously. She was afraid she and her children would soon fall into debt if she stayed in the apartment. Her mother, who is the "first wife" of her Kuwaiti father, could not help her. Her brother's family was already living with their mother, and there was no room. It is custom in this part of the world for sons to live with their families in their parents' home. Daughters are expected to live with the families of their husbands. At the same time, she was unwelcomed at her father's house. He now lived with his second wife, and besides, she said, her father was very sick with diabetes; she did not want to burden him.

Her mother also happened to be Egyptian. In Kuwaiti society, it is difficult sometimes for daughters of mixed marriages to find suitable or willing Kuwaiti families who permit their sons to marry them. Perhaps this was why she married an Egyptian in the first place. On the positive side, she liked her government job and was studying part-time at the university. She said she swam daily to stay strong. But she was very stressed about her financial predicament. At one point, she drew down her *niqab* to show her face. She was pale and gaunt, only a remnant of herself compared to the pictures she showed us of her in happier days, plump and wearing glamorous evening gowns to weddings she had attended. She was just one of the many women who fell victim to the imbalance of Kuwait's laws that discriminate against women. To me, she was an extraordinary representative of the pressures middle class women face in Kuwait in navigating the social welfare system and the rules that govern eligibility for the coveted Kuwaiti nationality.

The legal imbalance in the country, when it affects a woman so personally, can drive her into politics. This is what happened to Dr. Massouma Al-Mubarak, Kuwait's first female cabinet member who served as Minister of Planning in 2005. She also happened to be married to a Bahraini citizen. By the time she was asked to serve, Dr. Massouma was already well accomplished. Born in 1947, she studied in the United States where she obtained her Ph.D. in Political Science from the University of Denver. She raised her three children while studying abroad and credited her Bahraini husband, who was also studying at the time, for helping with the childrearing. While they were in the States, they did not focus on the Kuwaiti law that would deprive their children of Kuwaiti citizenship.

Upon returning, she taught Political Science at Kuwait University, eventually heading the Political Science Department. She also wrote a weekly column in the local Kuwaiti newspaper, *Al-Anba*. She had a lot to talk about as a young working mother, but also about her vast knowledge from living in the States where she learned so much about the women's movement, human rights, and women's rights. She soon became active in the campaign to secure women their right to vote in Kuwait. Her work in calling for an Amiri decree to amend Article I of the Electoral Law to allow women the right to vote caught the attention of the ruling family. The current Amir of Kuwait, then Prime Minister Sheikh Sabah Al-Ahmed Al-Sabah, asked her in 2005 to join the Cabinet as the Minister of Planning. This was a watershed event, but one that was not immediately embraced by many in the Kuwaiti legislature. When she walked into the National Assembly on June 19, 2005, to take her oath, loud and boisterous men refused to let her be heard. The only thing she could do was scream above the fray. And that is what she did and became Kuwait's first female to serve in the Cabinet.[cii]

Dr. Massouma was named Person of the Week on ABC News at the time, and was asked by then-ABC host Elizabeth Vargas why she wore the hijab. She responded, *"This cover doesn't affect what's under the cover,"* she said. *"I consider myself liberal. I consider myself futuristic. I consider myself activist."*[ciii] She is truly an example of how it is possible to be both Muslim and pursue equal rights under the law at the same time. During her tenure in government, Dr. Massouma played a significant role, for example, in prohibiting government ministries from discriminating against women by not hiring them on the basis of gender. While she opened the door for thousands of Kuwaiti women to work in the government today, she has not yet succeeded in providing her own children with Kuwaiti citizenship.

I had the pleasure of sitting next to Dr. Massouma at the home of one of her relatives gathered to celebrate the birth of a granddaughter. She came with her daughter and we talked about the difficulty of not having Kuwaiti citizenship. Dr. Massouma was very intelligent and humble about her achievements, and her daughter was quick to add Dr. Massouma was the "*best mom ever.*" I later saw her daughter at a wedding I attended. I noticed she was very much a part of Kuwaiti society and felt sad that she was not protected as a full citizen. Hopefully, the law that has discriminated against her accomplished mother will one day change so that she too can be a Kuwaiti citizen and pass it on to her own children.

# CHAPTER ELEVEN

## *Promoting America*

Kuwaiti citizenship also means opportunity in the business world. Until recently, partnerships with Kuwaiti business entrepreneurs were required in order for foreigners to establish companies in the country. American companies, like other foreign enterprises, had to work through complex legal relationships with Kuwaiti business families in order to succeed in the Kuwaiti marketplace. In light of Kuwait's move to provide a more open business environment, Doug's priorities as U.S. Ambassador became focused on introducing more American products and open new American businesses in the country. The State Department is tasked with protecting and creating jobs for U.S. citizens at home by working to expand markets overseas. This responsibility falls to U.S. ambassadors with the help of the U.S. Commerce Department and their Foreign Commercial Service officers working at U.S. Embassies.

According to the World Bank, the per capita income in this oil-rich emirate in 2014 was $43,600, placing Kuwait 22nd in per capita income in the world. The United States, meanwhile, was ranked 10th at the time with a per capita income of $54,500. With this much purchasing power in

Kuwait, it was worthwhile for American businesses to compete against the Chinese, Japanese, Korean, Turkish, Indian, Russian, European, and other foreign nationals also seeking a share of Kuwait's financial largess. Thus, encouraging U.S. businesses to enter the Kuwaiti market, highlighting the quality of American products and services, and promoting American businesses through events like grand openings and new product launches was an important duty of the U.S. ambassador.

American brands are very popular in Kuwait. I think just about every American restaurant chain is in Kuwait, from *Cheesecake Factory* and *Shake Shack* to *Texas Roadhouse* and *Pinkberry*. Even the upscale grocery store *Dean & DeLuca* is there. There are also plenty of American clothing stores like *American Eagle* and *Gap* as well as houseware stores like *Williams and Sonoma* and *Pottery Barn*. Kuwait had 82 *Starbucks Coffee* stores when I was there, making it one of the most popular franchises. With such a heavy presence in Kuwait, Starbucks CEO Howard Schultz and his wife Sheri came to visit Kuwait in January 2015. Kuwaiti businessman Mohammed Alshaya, who first introduced Starbucks to Kuwait, invited them and hosted a dinner in their honor at his home to which both Doug and I were invited.

It was amazing to hear both Schultzes talk about the importance of corporate social responsibility, given their reach across the world. They talked about their efforts to promote environmental awareness, improve the lives of coffee farmers, and provide opportunities for personal growth and education for their employees, including the baristas who serve the coffee. Alshaya showed off his business acumen by focusing on efforts to open more Starbucks stores in the region, including in Turkey, Azerbaijan, Russia and Kazakhstan. Alshaya, who studied at the Wharton Business School, ran a very diverse and successful enterprise far beyond just managing Starbucks franchises. His company has interests in areas ranging from real estate, hotels, cars, to a wide variety of retail and restaurant franchises, and he has expanded his business interests well beyond Kuwait.

His corporation had fast become the largest private sector employer in Kuwait. He welcomed talent and seemed happy whether it came from a man or a woman, a Kuwaiti or a non-Kuwaiti. He focused on who could do the job best. Certainly, he was an example of what could be achieved in Kuwait with a good education and an appetite for risk. He also certainly knew how to serve the best of the best when it came to entertaining in his home. The dinner consisted of five courses including the most tender filet mignon I had ever tasted. But what attracted my attention most were the ten carefully groomed and white-gloved servers divided on either side of the table. In perfect harmony, they laid plates of exquisitely presented food. For me, this was a whole new level of hospitality, well beyond what I have seen at diplomatic dinners. A dinner for the same number of guests at the ambassador's residence was normally a three-course meal served by a staff of two. The biggest difference, however, is our china, issued by the U.S. Government, which is embossed in gold with the great seal of the United States, and this for many, is reason enough to come to the home of the U.S. ambassador.

To my delight, Alshaya invited us to dinner again the following year. This time we met Todd Graves, the founder and CEO of the Raising Cane's restaurant chain that originated in Baton Rouge, Louisiana. Graves had come to Kuwait to open his company's first restaurant outside the United States. The idea of opening a Raising Cane's outside the United States was the result of a chance meeting between Graves and Alshaya in Texas. Alshaya had been holding open an empty space in Kuwait's famous Avenues Mall specifically for a chicken restaurant. Raising Cane's unique brand caught his attention. The rest is history and the restaurant has since become a huge success, demonstrated in the long lines I saw outside the restaurant. Alshaya also plans to open Raising Cane's restaurants in Saudi Arabia.

At the dinner, Alshaya asked Doug and me to participate with Todd Graves the next day in the grand opening of Kuwait's first Raising Cane's restaurant. It was particularly interesting for me to participate in this opening because I was able to meet some of the young Raising Cane's employees from Louisiana and Texas. They travelled to Kuwait and stayed about a month to teach local staff how to operate the restaurant. They included the kitchen staff as well as the managers. These young Americans were all very excited to be in Kuwait and were very happy they had such an amazing opportunity. They were thrilled to take pictures with their U.S. ambassador as well. They had each been carefully selected in the States for their skills, and many planned to travel later to Saudi Arabia to open Raising Cane's franchises there as well.

It seemed to me that this was a mini exchange program between the Middle East and the United States. This exchange program, however, was providing opportunity for a part of American society that does not often get to travel. These young Americans, many of whom had crossed the Atlantic for the first time, would return to the States with a whole new perspective of the world, especially of the Middle East. Many Americans from across the United States also live in Kuwait and manage the numerous U.S. businesses in the country. This is how many of these franchises maintain their brands to their original standards. Meeting these Americans living abroad highlighted for me how our economy today is truly global. Today there are so many more chances for people to pursue an international lifestyle. Being a diplomat is certainly not the only way to see the world.

The social impact of bringing in western companies to the region is also significant. Family style restaurants, like Raising Cane's, are changing the ways local families go out. More and more Saudi and Gulf families are enjoying going out to eat a meal together. In Kuwait, women and children were now less likely to peel off to more separate, curtained-off "family" sections in restaurants as they did in the past. Since these franchise restaurants in Kuwait typically offer only open seating, families are choosing more often to stay together in full sight rather than abiding by strict gender separation practices, at least at these American fast food restaurants.[civ]

There are a number of fabulously wealthy Kuwaiti business families like Alshaya bringing foreign franchises and other businesses into Kuwait. Many have gotten very wealthy because, for a long time, the only way for a foreign company to operate in Kuwait was to partner with a Kuwaiti sponsor. These merchant families have over the years benefited immensely from a law mandating that a Kuwaiti national own at least 51 percent of a foreign company operating in Kuwait. Some Kuwaitis, like Alshaya, are actively involved in these partnerships. Others have gotten rich by doing practically nothing except signing their names to a partnership for which they were guaranteed 51 percent of profits. The foreign business partner who did all the work often received only 49 percent.

Not many U.S. companies would want to sign a deal in which they would only receive less than half of their profits, and so over the long run, this sponsorship policy has impeded attracting foreign businesses to Kuwait. Because the Kuwaiti government would like to encourage foreign investment and promote greater private sector employment, the government has recently loosened its foreign ownership laws in some sectors. This is reflective of the Amir's desire to transform Kuwait into a financial and commercial hub. As of 2015, the government now allows as much as 100 percent foreign ownership in some sectors of the economy.

Among the most profitable businesses for the United States is Kuwait's purchase of American automobiles, spare parts and aircraft. Selling cars and other American manufactured products is critical to preserve and create jobs in the States and American cars happen to be wildly popular in Kuwait. Kuwaitis especially like to drive Ford, Dodge, and Chevy pickup trucks, great icons of American culture. Kuwaitis are also in love with American muscle cars like Mustangs and Camaros, and I saw a lot of these hot rods on the road as well.

Of course, Kuwaitis also have their share of Lamborghini and Ferrari sports cars. I saw a great deal of personal expression behind the wheel in Kuwait but we wanted to see Kuwaitis drive American cars, so when Doug received his first invitation to participate in the local launching of the 2015 Cadillac Escalade, he immediately accepted. This was actually Doug's first official event in Kuwait as it came the day after he presented his credentials on September 16, 2014.

I was also invited to attend this glamorous event held in the Prestige Ballroom in Kuwait's largest and most extravagant mall known as *The Avenues*. I recall feeling particularly impressed, as I had never attended a business event with so much pizzazz. Under a ceiling of sparkling lights, we were directed to sit in the front row on a white couch. We then proceeded to watch an artist throw glitter onto a large black velvet cloth to create his own image of an Escalade SUV that glowed under the fluorescent lighting. An aura of fantasy pervaded the room but then Doug was asked to come up to address the audience and brought the audience back to reality. He delivered a short speech in Arabic praising Cadillac's luxury brand. A barrage of local paparazzi then began taking photos of us. That was my first experience with the media. Later I would get used to being somewhat of a local celebrity, especially when I accompanied Doug.

The following month, the U.S. Department of Commerce officer at our embassy launched the second annual *"Discover America Week"* in Kuwait. I tagged along and participated with Doug in ceremonial ribbon cuttings opening several U.S. franchises and introducing new American brands. We decided that we made a bigger impression together as a couple at these events. Doug had also noticed that his Instagram account seemed to always register more "likes" when we both appeared in pictures, so he saw it was advantageous to have me along sometimes. Our first opening was the Sultan Center, a popular grocery store chain in Kuwait that carries more than 6,000 U.S. products. We met the predominantly Lebanese management of Sultan Center and shared a nice meal after cutting the ribbon.

We talked about the importance of taking care about what you eat to maintain a healthy weight but despite this, two huge steak dinners with mashed potatoes and vegetables were placed in front of us. This was after all how they thought Americans like to eat.

During our visit the following year at the Sultan Center for the third annual *Discover America Week*, we were pleased to see the grocery store promote more health food products. From organic fruits and vegetables to quinoa and coconut water, it was great to see more healthy food available to Kuwaitis, known to suffer from obesity and diabetes (more on that later). I also took the chance to ask the management if they could stop using corn oil in their hummus. I noticed their packaged hummus tasted different and discovered they were using corn oil as one of their ingredients. Hummus is the popular Middle Eastern dip made from cooked mashed garbanzo beans, garlic, tahini (sesame paste), and lemon. Olive oil is often drizzled before serving, but there is no corn oil in the traditional recipe. Although many Lebanese run the store, they were not the ones preparing the food behind the counter. Non-Arab expatriates unfamiliar with this popular dip made the food. Within a few weeks, I was pleased to find that the ingredients on the hummus packages were changed. The company management had made sure that their hummus was made with olive oil. It tasted a lot better. Such is the influence of the wife of the U.S. ambassador.

The next day, we opened a U.S. Education Fair in Kuwait. This is a huge business for U.S. colleges and universities. Private companies arrange fairs throughout the year, bringing dozens of U.S. colleges and universities from across the United States to Kuwait. Many Kuwaiti students receive full scholarships from the Kuwaiti government based on their grade point average, making them full paying students and very attractive customers for schools across the United States. This has become an increasingly lucrative business for American institutions of higher education. As of February

2016, of the 32,000 Kuwaitis who opted to study abroad, over 11,600 Kuwaiti students were studying in the United States.[cv]

After the Education Fair, we visited the upscale *360 Mall* to open a hands-on U.S. family-friendly franchise called *"Make Meaning."* This franchise provides a cheerful venue for families to paint pottery, make candles, soap and glass trays together. Being in Kuwait, the staff was mainly composed of expatriates, most from the Philippines. They did a great job of singing Pharrell Williams' pop tune "Happy" as we walked in and did their best to create a bright and happy atmosphere for their customers.

There was an energetic blonde who told us she had moved her family from New York City to Kuwait to open the store. She stands to do very well; she had already scheduled 22 birthday parties within a two-month period. We ended the day at the *360 Mall* at an American Film Festival and watched *"Believe Again"* with Keira Knightly and Adam Levine, an endearing movie despite a few clips censored by Kuwaiti authorities.

The following evening, the U.S. embassy's senior Commercial Officer hosted a reception to promote United Airlines. United shuttled a lot of our U.S. military back and forth in addition to the thousands of Americans who live here. The route was particularly convenient because it was a direct flight between Dulles Airport in Washington, DC, and Kuwait. I was surprised when United decided to stop flying the route in January 2016 after more than 10 years. Apparently other international routes were found to be more promising, especially in view of the rising strength of regional companies like Emirates, Etihad, and Turkish Airlines. This was another reminder of global competition.

After the reception, we went to the Kuwait Car Museum where we saw a collection of antique cars that I think would impress even Jay Leno. In the parking lot, we paid homage to the American Corvette and Camaro. I had no idea that nitric oxide tanks could be placed in the back of these cars to increase air intake and produce greater speed. Racing cars like these are a huge pastime in Kuwait. You can hear the cars racing in the middle of the night along the Gulf Road or on other main drags in the city. I also met a few Kuwaiti women who liked to race; there is a women's club with some pretty tough women racing against the men. One young woman, in western clothing, told us, "Yes, I look like a woman now, but inside my car, I am just like them." She said she just wanted to win and go very, very fast!

The grand finale of *Discover America Week 2014* was a reception at the U.S. ambassador's residence, my new home. This is why U.S. ambassadors have big homes with a number of staff, including a professional chef. Since our residence was located on U.S. soil, we could also serve wine. This of course made our home a particularly attractive destination in an otherwise dry country where alcohol is not served in public. The weather by October had finally begun to cool after a long hot summer. Three U.S. Congressmen also happened to be in Kuwait that evening on their way to visit the U.S. Embassy in Baghdad to meet with Iraqi officials. Doug made sure to invite them to the reception so they could help promote U.S. business in Kuwait as well. They seemed to enjoy the evening and were pleased with the effort to attract Kuwaiti investment in America.

# CHAPTER TWELVE

*Pearls to Oil*

Trade and commerce aside, Kuwait's economy is fundamentally based on hydrocarbons. The oil industry is present everywhere and in a constant state of motion to discover and exploit new sources. Workers regularly set off explosions deep underground and test seismic responses to find new fields. Oil rigs are quickly moved to potential sites to drill possible new wells. When a new well is established, it is attached to a vast array of pipelines that direct oil to the port for export. If the oil is not designated for export, it is diverted to Kuwait's enormous oil refineries and petrochemical plants with their labyrinths of tall steel towers connected by twisting pipes and tubes. At night, they glow in the dark as though they were small cities in the desert.

I made sure to go along with Doug when he received an invitation from the Kuwait Oil Company (KOC) to visit its headquarters. KOC is located in Ahmadi, about 20 miles south of Kuwait City near the vast Burgan oil field, the second largest onshore oil field in the world. As we rode into the desert toward Ahmadi, the first thing we noticed was Saddam Hussein's legacy of destruction on Kuwait's oil fields. As his troops withdrew from Kuwait in 1991, they set fires to some

700 oil wells. There were still large black scorch marks across the desert reminding us that the earth cannot always return to its natural state after such a violent attack by man.

The invading Iraqi forces also destroyed most of the buildings and homes that had comprised the original town of Ahmadi. After the liberation of Kuwait in February 1991, KOC was determined to rebuild the town exactly as it had been before the 1990 attack. Kuwait's national pride depended on this. Ahmadi had once been the thriving planned village for the many western oil executives who came to Kuwait in the mid-1940's from Britain and the United States. Their families grew the town to include churches, schools, hospitals, gardens, and recreation centers. Today, foreign executives and their families no longer live in segregated communities like Ahmadi. Instead, they live dispersed throughout the country, leaving Ahmadi to evolve into a pleasant town known for its greenery.

A cultural remnant of the original Ahmadi village era is the Ahmadi Music Group (AMG), established in the 1950's to help oil executives and their families pass the time with familiar songs from home. Initially sponsored by KOC, it has become an independent organization that attracts a diverse group of professional and amateur singers and instrumentalists who live in Kuwait today. Under the energetic and visionary direction of Richard Bushman, the AMG performs choral works and fully staged operas. Richard conducts the AMG orchestra as well as the choir and his wife, Harriet Bushman, a highly accomplished concert pianist and composer, accompanies the choir. She also performs independently throughout the city. I had the opportunity to sing in the AMG chorus for George Bizet's *The Pearl Fishers* in March 2015 and Mozart's *Don Giovanni* in April 2016. It was an extraordinary and very unique experience to be on stage, dressed in colorful saris, with professional opera singers from Europe and elsewhere. They went through a competitive audition before being selected to perform in Kuwait and it was truly an honor to sing with them.

Back at KOC headquarters, Kuwait's seafaring past is beautifully remembered in a very large wooden model of an old Kuwaiti dhow that stands in the entrance hall. This symbol of Kuwait's history is found in most every Kuwaiti institution to remind people of those early days. KOC's model boat was particularly large and beautiful, and we gathered around it to take a moment to reflect. Our Kuwaiti hosts at KOC were eager to talk about the history of Kuwait, especially since we were so new to the country when we visited that day.

Kuwaitis are descendants of the Bani Utub tribe who migrated from the Nejd desert in the Arabian Peninsula in the mid-18th century and settled at the top of the Persian Gulf. When the Bani Utub arrived in this relatively active commercial location, they settled around a *kut* (fortress) that gave Kuwait its name. This territory had originally belonged to the Bani Khalid tribe that was the most powerful tribal clan in the area at the time, known for maintaining warehouses to store dry goods, weapons and ammunition. The Bani Khalid tribe also helped people make the *hajj* to Mecca from Iran and southern Iraq.[cvi] By 1752, the Bani Khaled's power and influence declined and the Bani Utub succeeded in gaining control of the area. The Al-Sabah, the ruling family of the Bani Utub, were chosen to administer and defend their settlement, and have ruled ever since.[cvii]

When the British began to include Kuwait as a stop along their caravan routes moving valuable exports from India westward to Aleppo, the port in Kuwait became more important. Eventually Kuwait became the logical alternative to Basrah when the port there was occupied temporarily by Persia in 1776.[cviii] Kuwait during that time began to grow wealthy and eventually could finance its own shipbuilding to transform itself into a seafaring nation.[cix] The British remained as Kuwait's staunch allies and provided protection from encroaching Saudi tribes. Later, in the 19th century, the British helped Kuwait avoid being absorbed into the Ottoman Empire. In return, the Kuwaitis gave the British an active role in their internal affairs, culminating in the arrival of a British Political Agent to Kuwait in 1904.[cx]

Kuwaitis sailed their fleet of dhows as far away as India and the east coast of Africa. They sailed safely hugging the shorelines, using two main trade routes. One route took the dhows north along the northern edge of the Gulf. They stopped in Basrah first to load harvested dates into their hulls, and then eastward to trade their cargo in ports along the coasts of Persia and Baluchistan. After arriving in southern India, the dhows would head back to Kuwait carrying much needed supplies, including wood to build more boats. The second route led the Kuwaiti dhows south around the coasts of Arabia as far as Aden, again carrying a full cargo of dates for trade. They would then sail down the coast of East Africa, including stops in Dar es Salaam and Zanzibar, to carry spices and timber back to Kuwait.[cxi]

Kuwaiti dhows were also used in the flourishing pearl industry in the Gulf. This was a grueling commerce, especially for the divers who had to withstand the sting of salty water as they swam deep under the sea on a single breath. Once they located pearl oysters on the seafloor, they brought them up to the surface for marketing. There were others who had roles in the pearl economy, including sea captains, sailors, cooks, and the all-important *"tawaweesh"* who determined the quality of the pearls to be sold. The most valuable pearls were considered "white gold," well before the discovery oil when "black gold" would bring the region much greater wealth. The Arabic word for pearl in its singular form is *"Lulu"* and in the plural form, *"Loulwa".*[cxii] Now I know why so many women in Kuwait are fondly named "Lulu" or "Loulwa."

As pearl fishers and sailors, Kuwaitis were considered far less xenophobic than their Arabian tribal neighbors.[cxiii] They were so entwined with trade in south Asia that many Kuwaiti families spoke Urdu as their second language.[cxiv] Some families sent their children to be educated in India. Kuwait even used the Indian Rupee as its currency until 1960. The strong south Asian presence in Kuwaiti culture is apparent to this day. You can see it in the vivid colors of women's kaftans known as *dera'as*. You can taste it in their cuisine, pungent with eastern spices of black pepper, cloves, cardamom, saffron, cinnamon, and nutmeg.

Change came by the early 20th century, as Kuwaiti merchants and sailors began losing business to modern transportation routes through the Suez Canal and to the more durable steamships. Pearl diving profits also began to dwindle as Japanese cultured pearls began to flood the market in the 1930's. Kuwait's seafaring economy was by then fading. In many ways, the discovery of oil rescued Kuwait from descending into serious poverty and decline.

In 1934, a partnership comprised of the British Petroleum Company and the Gulf Oil Company, an American company founded in Pittsburgh, received rights from Amir Sheikh Ahmed al-Jaber Mubarak al-Sabah to search for oil in Kuwait. Their concession was the size of the entire country, 6,800 square miles. Fortuitously, in 1938, the partnership struck oil in the Burgan field that proved to be the largest known pool of oil in the world at the time. Kuwait started producing oil on August 23, 1938, but World War II slowed production. Once the war was over, production increased rapidly.[cxv] A decade later, the discovery of oil in Saudi Arabia's Ghawar field put Kuwait's Burgan field in second place as the largest oil field in the world, but Kuwait was already well on its way to becoming a very wealthy nation.

In 1961, the ruling Al-Sabah family declared Kuwait's independence from the British and Kuwait became a full member of the United Nations in 1963.[cxvi] Fourteen years later in 1975, in an amicable and negotiated settlement with its American and British partners, Kuwait decided to nationalize its oil industry. The KOC became a parastatal corporation with the Kuwaiti government setting general oil policy and KOC making the business decisions. While KOC focuses on the business of oil exploration and production, it works under the umbrella organization of the Kuwait Petroleum Corporation (KPC), formed in January 1980. KPC is the managing entity of all aspects of Kuwait's oil industry. In addition to oil exploration and production, it is responsible for separate companies that refine oil, process petrochemicals, market, and transport the oil with a huge network of tankers. KPC strives to ensure that all these "K Companies" operate at the highest level of efficiency together.[cxvii]

When we were in Kuwait, KPC presided over oil production that was the tenth largest in the world. The country possessed the sixth largest oil reserves, totaling some 104 billion barrels.[cxviii] At our briefing at KOC during our visit on November 2, 2014, we learned Kuwait was producing about three million barrels of oil per day and was working to boost production capacity to about 4 million barrels per day by 2020. KOC authorities also talked about their research and exploration to access oil deeper beneath the earth's surface. The plan was to drill wells going as deep as 20,000 feet and use 3-D seismic technology to see what was there. Not long after our visit, however, oil prices began to plummet dramatically.

Even as oil prices began to drop in the fall of 2015, KOC's then-Chief Executive Officer, Hashem Hashem, told the press the following February that KOC still planned to have 120 oil rigs in service by 2016 compared with its 2015 force of 80. I wondered why Kuwait would continue to invest in pumping more oil in an energy market where prices were sinking. For one thing, KPC believes it is important to continue to invest even when the market is down. This way Kuwait is in a good position when the market goes back up. But the real reason Kuwait can afford to keep pumping is that it is able to do so relatively cheaply. Kuwait is one of the lowest cost energy producers in the world because at the Burgan field, the oil naturally flows to the surface.[cxix]

According to the Wall Street Journal (WSJ), the break-even point for the Kuwaiti government to cover its budget in May 2015 was at the price of $47.10 a barrel.[cxx] Kuwait's break-even point is much lower than Saudi Arabia where it must make $103 a barrel to break even.[cxxi] Analysts are generally more concerned about how Saudi Arabia, a much larger country with a larger population, will manage the downturn in oil prices. Kuwait, on the other hand, is better positioned to survive the undulating energy market. At the end of the 2014-15 fiscal year, for instance, Kuwait saw its sovereign wealth fund rise by $53 billion to a record $592 billion despite the decline in oil prices.

Although Kuwait was somewhat protected by the fact that it invested its wealth all over the world and was capable of living off returns on investments for years to come, the budget deficit in 2015-16 and the anticipated larger deficit in 2016-17 were forcing the country to restructure some of its social welfare policies. Streamlining the country's social welfare benefits was difficult, however, especially since Kuwaitis have become accustomed to having so much wealth available for so many years. In April 2016, for instance, Kuwaiti oil workers went on strike in opposition to decisions to cut some of their financial benefits as part of an overall austerity package. The government succeeded in making them return to work once it made clear that disrupting the flow of oil would lead to even worse consequences.

The country has always been concerned about its future and has long planned for ways to support its citizenry who depend on the welfare state in the event of changes in the oil market. Central to Kuwait's survival has been its sovereign wealth fund that dates back decades and is now one of the largest in the world. It is administered by the Kuwait Investment Authority (KIA), responsible for ensuring long-term investments using the financial reserves gained from Kuwait's oil revenues. Kuwaiti law requires that 10 percent of the country's revenues be set aside for investment in the sovereign wealth fund.[cxxii] A senior Kuwaiti investment officer told us over dinner once that had Saddam Hussein not invaded Kuwait in 1990 and destroyed the country, Kuwait's sovereign wealth fund might have been valued today as much as 1.5 trillion U.S. dollars. But as fate would have it, the country was forced to spend much of its wealth in the 1990's to rebuild its war-torn country. The high oil prices over the past several years, however, have helped Kuwait to make up for lost time. And while oil prices were down now, there was always the possibility that they would rise in the future. Kuwaitis would have to tighten their belts for now but as long as their investments remained robust, life should not be too painful. Total reliance on the welfare state will likely one day have its limits.

According to Kuwait's Central Statistical Bureau Labor Force Survey in 2015, the percentage of Kuwaiti citizens employed in the public sector was 87 percent of the total national labor force.[cxxiii] This number does not even include the Kuwaitis employed in the parastatal oil companies that would push this percentage even higher. The public sector's appeal is largely due to the significant advantages of working in the public sector over the private sector. Government jobs have traditionally paid more, for one thing. For example, there are not many private sector jobs that would provide an across the board pay raise of 25 percent like the one Kuwaiti public sector employees received in 2012.[cxxiv]

There are other incentives to work for the government including the generous pension system. Women have been able to retire as early as age 40 if they have worked for a minimum of 15 years. Men have been able to retire at 49 after 20 years of service.[cxxv] Now I understand why a Kuwaiti friend, much younger than I, described herself as "retired." I had initially thought she was too young to be retired, but she really was retired and receiving a pension providing more than enough for her to stay home and raise her three young children. Wisely, the Kuwaiti government plans to increase gradually the retirement age for men to age 55 and to age 50 for women by 2020.

Following our informative tour at KOC headquarters, we were invited to lunch held at what is known proudly as the KOC Oasis, a lovely man-made lake surrounded by green grass, flowers, and palm trees with an island shaped like the map of Kuwait. The oasis is located in the middle of the Burgan oil field and was built on reclaimed polluted land from the terrible 1991 oil spills. It is a great source of pride and now a haven for migrating birds. The purpose of the oasis is to demonstrate the resolve of the Kuwaiti people to overcome the environmental trauma the war inflicted upon them. At the oasis, we ate a sumptuous lunch in a traditional tent under purple glass chandeliers. The former CEO of KOC Hashem Hashem was our host.

We ended our visit to KOC with officials inviting the U.S. embassy to participate in KOC environmental programs. Part of KOC's mandate, Hashem said, is to protect the environment. The organization strives internally to instill the concept of environmental protection at all levels of oil production in Kuwait. Externally, KOC supports volunteer programs to promote a clean environment throughout Kuwait.

My son Zach and I participated in one of KOC's beach clean-ups several months later. We entered first a large tent where a stage was set up to host various puppet and theater groups to talk to the hundreds of school children about the importance of keeping their environment clean. Once we reached the beach to pick up the trash, however, we understood just how important raising awareness about pollution was. We had no idea the beach would be so dirty. We donned plastic gloves and picked up a lot of trash. There were baby diapers, people's discarded cans and other food products, layer upon layer of trash. We suspected that the sea was bringing much of the trash in, though there was plenty of evidence that picnickers were failing to clean up after themselves. We put it all in the blue plastic bags provided by KOC.

Everything was going well until the children arrived on the beach with their own plastic gloves and bags to pick up the trash. They quickly became distracted and within minutes, the beach was full of flying clear plastic gloves and blue plastic bags. Suddenly the trash grew exponentially. Zach and I decided to stay after all the children left, and we picked up as much trash as we could, including the plastic bags and gloves. As we trudged back up the beach, a KOC executive spotted us and gave us a beautiful glass plate in recognition of our hard work. We both felt good about doing something helpful, but we also could see that it was an uphill battle to get the message across not to throw trash on the beaches. I am pleased to say, however, that I would meet many in Kuwait who care a great deal about the need to protect Kuwait's beaches and marine life.

# CHAPTER THIRTEEN

## *Lifestyle Chain Reaction*

Living in such a tiny country, smaller than the State of New Jersey, producing enough oil to put it in the top ten list of oil producers in the world, made me also wonder about Kuwait's environment and people's health. Although the economic benefits from producing enormous amounts of petroleum were clear, pollution, as in industrial regions around the world, has become an unfortunate byproduct. Today pollution is causing health problems in the country and medical costs associated with treating them are soaring.

Pollution is not easy to talk about in Kuwait because petroleum production is the lifeline of the society. It is also easy to overlook, especially when looking across the Gulf's sparkling waters to admire Kuwait's attractive skyline. But if you look closely at the horizon, there is a distinct layered haze. Nearest the ground, the air can look slightly orange. Then it fades into a white haze before finally appearing blue at the very top. These layers are the result of several different processes. The orange is mostly dust and sand blown in from the Iraqi and Saudi deserts. This dust is heavy so it tends to settle on the lowest parts of the atmosphere. The white haze is a mixture of pollutants that are most likely from the burning of fossil fuels.[cxxvi]

In Kuwait, as in countries around the world, fossil fuel is burned driving cars, producing electricity for air conditioning, electronics, and lights, but in Kuwait, fossil fuel is also burned to extract oil from the desert and desalinate water to drink. An awful lot of fuel is burned in a relatively tiny space.

People who live in Kuwait are essentially breathing lots of dust and sand particles as well as pollutants from fossil fuels.[cxxvii] Like smoking, the introduction of foreign particles and chemicals into our lungs causes health problems. Ozone, Sulfur Dioxide, and Nitrous Oxide, all chemicals associated with air pollution, can cause asthma, increase the risk of cancer, cause heart problems, and lower life expectancy.

When I went to a doctor's appointment in Kuwait regarding allergies, the Arab American family practitioner, who obtained his medical degree from the States, talked at length about how he was diagnosing so many of his patients with asthma. He was having trouble convincing his Kuwaiti patients, however, to believe they had asthma. They simply could not fathom that the air they breathed would cause difficulties that would require using an embarrassing device like an inhaler. The doctor was clearly frustrated. He surmised that the air quality must be extremely bad in Kuwait since he was encountering so many cases of asthma. A medical study dated from 2012 stated that the prevalence of asthma in Kuwait was estimated to be 15% of adults and 18% of children. In comparison to the United States, these rates are high.[cxxviii] In the States, as of 2016, the asthma rates are 7.4 percent for adults and 8.6 percent for children.

I raise the issue of pollution because, in my role as the wife of the ambassador, I was asked to participate in campaigns to raise public awareness about health issues. Although Kuwaitis are very well off, there is a high degree of suffering that goes on in this tiny population of less than 1.3 million citizens. Cancer, cardiovascular disease, and asthma have increased more aggressively since the onset of oil production and pollution. Of course, these diseases also threaten the nearly three million expatriates who live here as well. I often thought about my own health in Kuwait because I knew I was also breathing the same dust and pollution. Learning more about air quality and environmental pollution in Kuwait is important, especially for those who make Kuwait their home.

Data, however, about air quality has not been fully available to the public in Kuwait. As a result, Kuwait has not been included in global pollution metrics. Other Gulf countries, meanwhile, have been providing data and their rankings have not been very good. Qatar ranked second most polluted country in the world per capita in the World Health Organization's 2014 global ranking. The United Arab Emirates was ranked eighth, and Bahrain was ranked tenth. It is not a stretch to imagine Kuwait would be in a similar category had international organizations been able to take a look at Kuwait's air quality data.[cxxix]

As a coastal country, Kuwait also suffers from marine pollution. Strong odors often waft from the Gulf onto the city streets from the tons of plastic bags, litter and sewage that find their way into the sea and slowly disintegrate. Eating local seafood favorites like *hamour* (grouper), *zubaidi* (pomfret), and shrimp become a little less appetizing when considering the reported chemicals and hospital refuse, including discarded medical equipment, dumped into the water. A U.S. embassy officer who followed environmental issues in Kuwait told me that he no longer ate local fish that fed in Gulf water since he had become aware of what these fish were feeding on. The staggering amount of treated and untreated sewage dumped into Kuwait Bay contains bacteria, fungi, worms and viruses that could pose health problems for humans such as cholera and other diseases.[cxxx] Since pollution in the sparkling blue Gulf waters is not always readily seen, people swim in the Gulf all the time. Public awareness is also needed with regard to the cleanliness of the water.

A pilot who flew over the Gulf into Kuwait one day told my husband he counted 53 oil tankers lined up to go to one of the numerous Kuwaiti offshore oil loading platforms.

That number is just in a single day. The problem is that many of these tankers spill oil into the sea, and this frequent oil spillage pollutes the Gulf waters. Dr. Abdul-Rahman Al-Awadi, Executive Secretary of the Regional Organization for the Marine Environment and a former Kuwaiti Minister of Health, once said, referring to the disastrous oil spills caused by the Iraqi invasion, "If we go on like this, we won't need a war to complete the destruction of our marine environment. Normal (tanker) operations will do it." Environmentalists generally blame the majority of oil spillage from tankers on negligence or mismanagement by the companies involved. They also believe that basic environmental standards are being ignored.[cxxxi]

Today, organizations like the Kuwait Institute for Science Research (KISR) are working hard to conduct the necessary research and provide the appropriate data to assist policymakers in preserving the environment. The country also established in 2015 the Kuwait Environment Police to help implement tougher laws. Authorities, including the Amir himself, understand the magnitude of the problems posed by pollution and are taking steps to educate the population. Educating the Kuwaiti public is most important because it has the power to demand a cleaner atmosphere and environment.

The March 2015 opening of Al-Shaheed Park, a project under the stewardship of the Amiri Diwan, the personal office of the Amir, is certainly a demonstration of the government's commitment to the environment. The park is a stunning urban green space comprised of almost 50 acres (200,000 square meters). It is Kuwait City's own Central Park with botanical gardens, a lake, outdoor theater, and walking and jogging paths. There is also a state-of-the-art habitat museum that educates people, especially youth, about the effects of pollution through interactive learning stations embedded in intricate displays of the country's diverse ecosystems. Still, there is much to be done. Kuwaitis not only have to ensure clean air and water, but they also have to address their lifestyle choices.

It is not just pollution that is behind the growing presence of non-communicable diseases in Kuwait. It is also the lifestyle brought on by great wealth. Kuwaitis have become less physically active with the acquisition of oil wealth. They no longer have to work as hard for a living as when they were pearl divers, shipbuilders, and traders. Nor do they have to do all the cooking and cleaning. Almost every home today has a cadre of foreign laborers to do the household chores. And it is very easy to order food directly to the home, thanks to Kuwait's plethora of western restaurant franchises and premier food delivery services. McDonald's, for instance, is available to deliver food to your doorstep 24/7.

With the majority of Kuwaiti adults travelling by car to and from their government office jobs and fulfilling their heavy social schedules, not a lot of focus has been given to physical activity. Kuwaiti social events typically involve generous buffets of delicious food or going out for fabulous restaurant meals together. Over time, Kuwaitis have simply begun to consume more calories than they burn. Like Americans in the States, Kuwaitis are also indulging at fast food restaurants, choosing from menus offering large portions of heavy and fried food. It absolutely amazed me as I drove around Kuwait to see the ever-increasing number of fast food restaurants being built. This new construction certainly supported what a local businessman told my husband at a dinner at our residence in April 2016: 70 percent of all new businesses in Kuwait revolved around food.[cxxxii] Not surprisingly, waistlines are now bulging, and the rate of obesity has soared in Kuwait as it has in much of the developed world.

When I started researching Kuwait before arriving in 2014, I was a little concerned that among the first things that popped up on the Internet was that the country had one of the highest levels of obesity in the world; according to a 2010 clinical study, an estimated one-third of all Kuwaiti adults were considered obese. Unfortunately, the problem has become worse. In 2014, the *Global Burden of Disease Study* ranked Kuwait the fourth most obese country on the planet. It said that 50 percent of women in Kuwait, along with women in Libya, Qatar, and Samoa, were considered obese. They noted particularly high rates of childhood obesity in Middle Eastern and North African countries, notably among girls. The problem is that obesity, which is reversible with more exercise and less eating, can lead to serious cardiovascular disease, cancer, diabetes, osteoarthritis, and kidney disease. The question has become for those involved in the Kuwaiti health care system, whether there are even enough doctors and hospitals to take care of an impending health crisis due to poor health stemming from obesity.

Among the most serious diseases associated with obesity is the rise in Type II diabetes, especially among children. Medical studies have indicated that the prevalence of Type II diabetes in adult Kuwaitis is spreading to children and adolescents. More children are dealing with serious complications from diabetes at younger ages. According to Dr. Sheila Magge with the Washington, D.C.-based Children's National Health System who spoke at Kuwait University in late January 2015, "If an adult was diagnosed around 70, complications would emerge when he or she reached the age of 80. Now if a child is being diagnosed at just 10 years of age, the complications are occurring earlier and the deterioration is happening faster. If you look forward, it could be a huge public health issue."[cxxxiii]

There are Kuwaitis who are trying to turn this alarming trend around. The Dasman Diabetes Institute, situated in the heart of the city overlooking the Gulf, is helping to lead the way out of this foreboding health crisis. Dasman's mission is "to prevent, control and mitigate the impact of diabetes and related conditions in Kuwait through effective programs of research, training, education, and health promotion." I toured this Institute with Doug in early 2015 with then-Director General, Dr. Kazem Behbehani, once a visiting professor at Harvard Medical School and former official of the World Health Organization. Dr. Behbehani also took us to Dasman's national Genome Center that contains one of the country's largest computers with impressive high-end storage servers and network services. A treasure trove of information about the Kuwaiti population exists in this center. With centuries of tribal custom that has promoted intermarriage within families, the data inside Dasman's computers must hold a very unique tale of human genetics. The Genome Center's work has already helped isolate specific genes that play a role in the pathogenesis of diabetes and obesity in the Kuwaiti population.[cxxxiv] This, according to Dr. Behbehani, will assist in how this disease can be medically treated and in understanding how the condition is inherited from parents.

In addition to research, the Dasman Institute is a firm believer that prevention is the best strategy to confront obesity and diabetes, and it has launched a wide campaign to promote healthy living. In many ways, Dasman has also become an incubator for cultural change. With Kuwaiti government support, Dasman representatives have gone into schools throughout the country to test Kuwaiti children for diabetes and record their results. Their goal is to try to search for reasons why they are seeing such high rates of obesity and diabetes in the country. They want to know if there is something in the culture that is behind the elevated rates of the disease; whether there are any behavioral issues they need to know about; and to quantify any increased risk from genetics. This is part of their effort to provide more personalized medical care tailored more closely to the needs of the community, as well as the individual.

Dasman also invites groups of students to the Institute to educate them about the dangers of diabetes and obesity. This program is funded by a grant from the U.S. Department of State's Middle East Partnership Initiative (MEPI) that funds programs that promote positive change in society. I had the opportunity to attend a couple of these sessions at Dasman in February 2016. The first was for a group of high school boys from a local private English-Arabic bilingual school. The lectures were in English and were very direct about the dangers of not exercising and the need to eat right. The boys appeared to grasp it, although the presenters felt that they were not always accorded the level of attention they would have liked. It may be difficult, I thought, for these Arabic-speaking boys to function in a second language. They were also teenagers and, unfortunately, I felt it was assumed they would misbehave. The culture is hard on young boys, in my opinion.

The final component of the awareness program engaged the boys directly on what they would like to do in their future careers. I found this particularly effective. Boys growing up in Kuwaiti families are treated at very early ages as authority figures in the family. They often accompany their mothers to the shopping malls and represent them in any dealings in the public domain. It is difficult to know how much real training they have before they are expected to act like grown men. I thought having senior Dasman doctors, scientists, and administrators make themselves available to explain to the boys all the steps required to get where they were today very instructive. It helped the boys understand how important it was to study and work hard to realize their own career goals and potential.

Following the boys' program, I sat in on the awareness program presented to a younger group of girls from a Kuwaiti public school. The program was in Arabic, and the teacher appeared very upbeat and interactive. She went through the material as if it were a memorization game, reviewing the causes of diabetes but without, it seemed to me, the same passion about how devastating this disease could be. It seemed as though it was just another lesson, rather than an effort to highlight the real dangers of diabetes. I asked how many girls had family members who were affected with diabetes, and nearly all their hands went up. In a way, it seemed as though the Arabic teacher did not want to frighten the girls. Many grow up with the disease or have close relatives who have it. Diabetes has become a part of life for them. In many ways, these young girls don't really question it or think that they can do things to prevent it.

For Dr. Bahareh Azizi, a U.S. citizen of Kuwaiti origin educated at Georgia Tech and former Head of Basic Research at Dasman, there is no room for complacency about this disease. She is particularly alarmed by the rates of Type II diabetes. According to Dr. Azizi, the prevalence of Type II diabetes has reached 23.1 percent in Kuwait. This means that one in five Kuwaitis will likely get the disease if they don't start changing their habits toward food and exercise. It is truly a silent killer, and a massive public campaign is required to call Kuwaitis to action. She lauded the Susan G. Komen Foundation for its success in campaigning against breast cancer in the United States and wished there could be the same type of effort against diabetes in Kuwait. She feels her efforts to raise awareness in Kuwait have been hampered by the fact that there are so many restaurants in Kuwait, making it so easy to choose the wrong foods and eat way too much of it.[cxxxv]

Kuwaitis are, however, getting the message to do something about their health. For one thing, the health and wellness industry is flourishing, especially among the educated and wealthy elite. I spoke to a personal trainer from New Zealand who had worked in Kuwait for four years. She could attest to the fact that many Kuwaitis she encounters are very interested in leading healthier lives. They face many social challenges, though. When she works with her clients, she requires them not to eat in restaurants for a period of three months, as this is the hardest habit to break. Many Kuwaitis also have cooks at home, and they find it difficult to retrain them to prepare healthy food with less fat, and served in smaller portions with more fruits and vegetables. The cooks feel it is their duty to prepare generous meals, especially when entire families gather in the homes where they work. My husband and I had this experience with our own brilliant Filipino chef who worked in our residence. We had to persuade him to no longer bake his delicious bread or his other tempting dishes high in carbohydrates. In the beginning, it was hard to convince him that "less" is "more" in terms of health, but it was equally hard for us to establish these rules in the first place. We happily broke them whenever we had guests for dinner. Our chef made incredible desserts as well. To explain the extra pounds, many diplomats will say that part of their duty is to eat for their country.

There are plenty of gyms and yoga centers in Kuwait. There seems to be something for everyone. When I arrived, I visited several gyms to find one I liked. I considered briefly attending an all-women's gym on the top floor of a nearby upscale mall. I quickly abandoned the option when I walked in and found all the shades drawn over the large windows that would have provided a stunning 180-degree view of the city. I felt so claustrophobic without the natural sunlight. I asked whether it was absolutely necessary to keep the shades down, and the staff said it was because their female Kuwaiti clients had complained that men were viewing them with binoculars from apartment buildings nearby. There were plenty of women wearing their hijab and exercising, and I was happy they felt comfortable but it was not the place for me. In the end, I chose the most western gym in town; it was co ed and offered the exercise classes I was familiar with.

Healthy food is also becoming popular. In March 2016, I accompanied my husband to the grand opening of a new grocery store in Kuwait called *Approved Market*, a brand new health food store based on the Whole Foods concept. It is on a much smaller scale but if the concept takes off, it could be a huge economic opportunity in Kuwait. The U.S. ambassador was invited to open the store because 70 percent of the products sold were from the United States, and the store deals directly with more than 20 U.S. suppliers. The owner of *Approved Market* is Fahad Al-Yahya, famous for having more than 400,000 Instagram followers on his *@TheDietNinja* account. He has proselytized for years on the importance of eating well and exercising. Of course, he also markets health food products on his Instagram account since he is a business entrepreneur as well. As we were about to depart the opening, we met Fahad's mother. She appeared in a fashionable black *abayya* and draping black hood to cover her hair. She was stunning, tall and beautiful. She was clearly very proud of her son and fortunate to have access to his advice, advice I wish could be made available to all Kuwaiti women.

While doing physiotherapy for a minor sports injury, I could not help but notice hanging on the wall of the Fawzia Sultan Rehabilitation Institute in Kuwait the results of a 2009-2011 survey of over 2,000 patients. The results indicated that "Kuwaiti women reported having significantly higher pain intensity, greater number of pain sites, longer duration of pain, and more gradual onset of pain, taking more regular medication and having had more previous surgeries than Kuwaiti men or non-Kuwaiti women or men." The findings highlighted the potential role of cultural factors and their contribution to chronic pain and medical condition in Kuwait, as well as gender-specific implications stemming from cultural influences. The study recommended strategies to modify the specific lifestyle factors leading to this increased incidence of pain among Kuwaiti females and to support Kuwaiti women in preventing and managing their pain.

For me, this sounded like an urgent call for Kuwaiti women to no longer accept that it is God's will that they live in pain. It is common to hear people in Kuwait, and elsewhere in the Muslim world, to say things like "*Alhamdulillah*" and "*Inshallah.*" These words, as beautiful and as popular as they are, pertain to the belief that everything is God's will. Their utterance reflects acceptance that things that happen to us are out of our hands. However, there are Muslims who believe that actively maintaining good health is something for which people should accept individual responsibility. For one thing, better health enables good Muslims to practice their faith better in the first place. On the website "The Religion of Islam," a contributor wrote that "a truly health conscious person blends diet, nutrition and exercise with the remembrance of God and an intention to fulfill all their religious obligations." While such religious obligations include wearing modest clothing for women, this does not appear to have stopped Muslim women from exercising. I see more and more women in the gym wearing a sports hijab and working out. Their discipline makes them excellent athletes and underscores that Muslim women should not use the need for modesty as an excuse not to exercise. Encouraging greater physical activity and introducing active sports into the daily lives of Kuwaiti women is certainly one way to improve women's health in Kuwait. An active lifestyle, however, must begin in childhood.[cxxxvi]

Providing equal access to women in sports on school playgrounds and college campuses has become increasingly important in Kuwait, but young women also need the support of their families. The daughter of a Kuwaiti friend tried to start a rowing team when she attended Kuwait University a decade ago. It did not go unnoticed that her daughter was looking great from all the exercising she was doing and so 15 other girls joined her team. When the team was invited to participate in a competition, however, none of the young women's parents would allow their daughters to participate. Some of the mothers rationalized that they did not want their daughters having wide shoulders. Others made it clear they did not want them to be seen wearing shorts in public.[cxxxvii] Needless to say, the parents helped put an end to the rowing team that deprived these young women of great exercise and experiencing team sportsmanship.

Many of these girls came from public schools where physical education, "P.E.", involved not much more than putting on a uniform and doing about five minutes' worth of activity.[cxxxviii] Some girls tried to get out of doing anything at all by claiming they had their periods, which, in this part of the world, is an acceptable reason. I remember when I had my period as a teenager on my exchange program in Turkey, I was forbidden from going swimming or doing much activity at all. Instead I was expected to stay in the house and wait for it to be over. Having grown up in the States during the era of Title IX that gave girls and boys equal access to federal funding for sports, this attitude towards a girl's monthly menses was completely alien to me. In the States, girls were being taught that we could achieve physical fitness just like the boys, regardless of our gender.

In Kuwait's private schools, it is a different story for girls. Like the boys, girls participate in an active sports program, travel to other countries to play against other teams, and yes, wear shorts in public. Certainly, the presence of these private schools throughout Kuwait City has provided Kuwaitis and the expat community in Kuwait an important outlet for women's sports. In public schools, only boys in Kuwait participate in sports like volleyball, soccer, and gymnastics.[cxxxix] Thus the public education system could do more to improve women's health by providing a more robust athletic program for girls during the school day.

This is precisely what drives Balsam Al-Ayoubi, a former national and professional fencing champion in Kuwait. I had the opportunity to meet this tall, attractive and elegantly dressed Kuwaiti athlete during a local TedX Talk held at the Kuwait Institute of Science and Research (KISR) in the suburb of Shuwaikh on March 24, 2016. Her personal story of struggle as an athlete in a society that did not value her talent was compelling. Each time she talked about her childhood, having grown up in an athletic family in which both her mother and father were active in sports, she would begin to cry. First, she would think of her deceased father who lovingly encouraged her to be athletic. And then she would think about how no one had explained to her as a child that, although she grew up competing with her brother on the playground and in the family home on the same level, she would not be accorded the same chances as him to pursue sports in the larger community. Now she wants to make sure that no Kuwaiti girl who has a passion for sports goes through what she did. This is a big undertaking.

Today Balsam has dedicated herself to encouraging youth sports programs in Kuwait with an emphasis on girls. She spends her time teaching in workshops and programs throughout the country, in schools and universities as well as in local sports clubs. She believes strongly that athletics builds character and enables those who practice sports to be focused, disciplined, and self-reliant, excellent skills to possess in life. Balsam knows first-hand how they have helped her become one of the few female professional athletes in the Gulf, and she truly wants to teach these qualities to others. Sports are also a means to *empowerment* and *gender equality*; two terms Balsam only learned when she was selected to be an Ashoka fellow in 2009 at the age of 32. The Ashoka organization connects people in over 70 countries who have a passion to change the world, like Balsam's desire to change social attitudes toward women's participation in sports in her country. Hopefully, her efforts will encourage a more physically active female population in Kuwait in the future, where mothers, aunts, sisters, and daughters will choose to live healthier lives and teach their loved ones to do so as well.

# CHAPTER FOURTEEN

## *Catching Up*

Lunch at an ambassador's residence was a chance for open and frank dialogue over a three-course meal. At our house, my seat was to the right of the head guest when I participated. The head guest would sit across from Doug who preferred to sit in the middle of a large table with the remaining guests filling the table to both ends. We tried to seat together people we thought would have a good conversation. Protocol was always tricky, but we wanted people to feel comfortable enough to talk openly. Young social media gurus, entrepreneurs, scientists, women activists, business executives, politicians, and human rights advocates have all been guests and discussions have most always been fascinating.

When a senior Washington visitor came for lunch in April 2015 to discuss the Kuwaiti economy, however, I noticed there was some anticipation. Our guests included successful Kuwaiti businessmen and senior government officials. Kuwait, it seemed at the time, was falling behind its peers in the Gulf in terms of public infrastructure and private sector development. Everyone was wondering how Kuwaitis could possibly catch up, how they could get the government to focus on improving the country's transportation network, its schools, and hospitals, all currently controlled by the government sector. How could Kuwaitis cut through their bureaucracy to invest their vast wealth better and develop the country so that it too could shine like its emirate neighbor in Dubai?

During the lively conversation, Kuwaiti businessmen railed at the government's failure to produce a clear vision of Kuwait's future. Without a vision, a roadmap that enabled Kuwaiti investors to know where the country was going, these businessmen revealed they were choosing not to invest their money in their own country. Instead they were investing in Europe and the United States where their investment promised a greater return. With so much Kuwaiti money leaving the country, private money has not focused on improving Kuwaiti infrastructure. These businessmen found it too difficult to tangle with the government to get construction projects off the ground.

Big business families wanted to invest in their country, but were not sanguine about Kuwait's future. The businessmen at the table admitted that even with the 25 years since Kuwait's liberation from Saddam Hussein's forces, they still did not feel secure. Hopefully these business families will overcome their insecurities and help expand the private sector. Private sector growth is key in creating new jobs and opportunities to jumpstart the economy. It will also inspire a sense of national pride and purpose. While Kuwait's oil-rich budget can afford to pay the welfare subsidies to its people well into the future, Kuwaitis themselves are growing wary of their country's tired infrastructure and their over-dependence on the public sector for their livelihood.

According to Lidia Qattan in *Rulers of Kuwait*, Amir Abdullah Al-Salem Mubarak Al-Sabah, who ruled during the period 1950 to 1965, set the stage for Kuwait to become a benevolent welfare state. His motives were pure when he said, "The wealth of this country, granted by God to its people, must always and forever be used for the betterment of their living condition and help them to achieve their noble ends in life."[cxl] In his view, national wealth included the country's land.

Thus, the state began to buy up land and eventually enacted a law in 1952 declaring that a full 97 percent of the country's land was *Aradhy Al-Amiriyah*, meaning *"land belonging to the state."* Much of the economic stasis, according to our business friends at the table, comes from the fact that the Kuwaiti government today controls almost all of the land and the resources associated with it, including, of course, oil.

Because land is so scarce and expensive, many private businesses must rely on leasing arrangements with the government over which they have little control. When businesses do not own the land, they are not keen to invest. They never know when the government might change its mind on use of the land, and they do not want to risk investing in infrastructure that they eventually could lose. Some Kuwaiti businessmen who own private schools in Kuwait, for example, are reluctant to expand or modernize the infrastructure of their schools because they sit on government-leased land. Negotiations with the government to purchase land or lease adjacent land for renovations and expansion are arduous and can take years. It is easy to see the deleterious effects of this policy on private education, particularly in the schools that were established 50 years ago. Although their western administrators and teachers strive to provide the latest educational practices, it is easy to spot the older facilities that they must work in. Surely in such a wealthy country, parents should be able to send their children to state-of-the-art schools.

In addition to rundown school facilities, the Kuwaiti businessmen complained about the lackluster state of Kuwait's international airport and airline. At the very mention of Kuwait International Airport, there was audible despair and visible embarrassment. All, including myself, were familiar with the shabby appearance of Kuwait's only international airport. It was disorganized and easy to feel lost in the sea of humanity traveling between the East and West. Airports and airlines in this part of the world are a great place to show off national wealth and success. The international airports in the United

Arab Emirates and Qatar are much more impressive and Emirates, Etihad and Qatar Airlines have done an excellent job in expanding their market and becoming top international airlines. Kuwait Airways trails well behind but it is trying to catch up. The airline recently purchased 10 new Boeing 777-300ER aircraft that will seriously boost the airline as well as the bottom line of this key American company.[cxli]

There was suddenly an overwhelming concern among our Kuwaiti guests that if Kuwait were to renovate its public infrastructure all at once, the country would go into spiraling debt. If so much cash was put into so many projects at once, the burden on the budget would be too great. This sense of fear that financial resources might run out was fascinating and yet very real due to the very strong dependence of the population on the social welfare system. This underlying fear is pervasive and can explain some of Kuwait's overall hesitation to invest and push itself forward.

At this point in the conversation, the senior government guests at the table jumped in. They assured everyone that there were in fact Kuwaitis in government who understood that their role went beyond handing out subsidies. The government was also responsible for creating an environment that encouraged the private sector. They saw the need for government to create jobs for their people as well as improve infrastructure in their country. One youthful government official assured our group that the government was actually working very hard to create more private sector opportunities for youth. The Kuwaiti government was employing younger and western-educated Kuwaitis to help create opportunities, especially for young entrepreneurs. In his view, the problem was that these government efforts were not being well publicized.

Well then, asked a Kuwaiti businessman, why doesn't the Prime Minister do a weekly press briefing? Why can't the government make the business community aware of these plans so that it may be more inclined to invest in the country? Clearly there was an appetite for private-public sector discourse and the concern about the need to create more jobs to accommodate Kuwait's young population. Twenty-five percent of Kuwait's population is under 15 years old[cxlii] and there may not be enough jobs for Kuwait's future generations.

A senior executive with a Lebanese construction company who has worked for nearly a decade in Kuwait was not optimistic when he talked about the trials of working in Kuwait's ballooning public sector. He said that when he first started reporting to work at a Kuwaiti government facility known as the Kuwait Ministries Complex, he could park right near the front door. Today, parking places for some 8,500 employees surround the complex. He now must park several lots away from the entrance. Even though the government has more workers, in his opinion, less work is getting done and at an even slower rate. He wondered how much longer the country could function with so much bureaucracy inhibiting productivity.

Kuwaitis who do have good jobs in the government are also concerned about the future of public service, especially about youth being able to find jobs. A Kuwaiti woman working in a public university told me she felt "older" employees in their "fifties" in senior positions should not stay long. They should retire to make room for people in their forties, such as herself. Once she was promoted, she promised she would not stay long so her own children would also have opportunities to work in the public sector. Kuwaitis are beginning to realize that the government is not going to be able to employ everyone forever and are now thinking about their own children's future.

Fortunately, there are motivated private citizens in Kuwait who are stepping up to develop ways to help youth find meaningful jobs outside the government to keep them engaged and inspired. There are several organizations dedicated to opening doors for youth in Kuwait. Among them are INJAZ Al-ARAB, TMKEEN, and LOYAC. These organizations are working largely in the private sector and act as agents of change to help to address societal challenges in

Kuwait as well as in the region that affect youth most of all. INJAZ Al-ARAB groom youth to think independently and creatively to become entrepreneurs and create businesses on their own. It is a non-profit organization that focuses on youth education and training in workforce readiness, financial literacy and entrepreneurship across the Arab world. It is part of the Junior Achievement Organization from the United States and currently operates in 15 countries including Algeria, Bahrain, Egypt, Jordan, Kuwait, Lebanon, Morocco, Oman, Pakistan, Palestine, Qatar, Saudi Arabia, Tunisia, United Arab Emirates, and Yemen.

Entrepreneurship is a wonderful elixir for youth. When you see the faces of youth who are involved in their own inventions and ideas to introduce into the local marketplace, there is so much pride. I had the chance to see this directly when I accompanied my husband to the December 2014 Eighth Annual Awards Ceremony of INJAZ Al-ARAB Young Entrepreneurs Competition held at the Regency Hotel in Kuwait. Students from across the Middle East region came to Kuwait to exhibit their original products to compete for top recognition. It was very exciting to meet all the teams and see their brilliant inventions. That year the theme of the inventions was that they had to use recycled materials in order to compete.

As I walked from exhibit to exhibit, eager young students wanting to talk about their ideas and products pulled me into their booths. I recall Kuwaiti students were particularly ingenious with their idea of assembling modern-looking furniture from old car parts, perfect for Kuwaitis who adore the automobile. Steel tables with interesting legs of various car parts and couches made from car seats were among their creative ideas. A group of young women from Egypt dressed in Pharaonic robes for effect, recycled papyrus into reusable household items they proudly displayed in their booths. There were small tables, plates, cups and many more useful things made of recycled materials.

Once the students gathered on stage to learn who won the competition, I could not help but notice a group of girls from Saudi Arabia participating in the competition. At first, I felt sad for these poor girls because they were completely covered in a black *niqab*, veils with small slits for their eyes. Although the audience was visible to them, they were anonymous to us. But then my husband pointed out how admirable it was these girls were allowed to compete in such a public event. The only way they could possibly travel away from their homes and be present at the competition was to be fully covered and hidden from view. I was beginning to understand that the veil enabled women and girls to participate in public and then appreciated how important it was for these Saudi girls to have the same opportunity as the Saudi boys' team. Girls, like boys, also need to learn to be creative and think entrepreneurially. These Saudi girls achieved their goal but in a way I had not imagined.

Another organization, TMKEEN, founded in Kuwait, also aims to encourage entrepreneurship by creating programs that help educate, inform, and inspire youth. Since 2012, TMKEEN, meaning *empowerment*, has sponsored Youth Empowerment Symposiums annually. I attended the November 2015 conference and met U.S. entrepreneurial luminaries Ian McNish, a co-founder of LinkedIn, Mark Kawano, co-founder and CEO of Storehouse, and Libby Gill, who owned her own company specializing in PR and branding. They were present to give inspiring talks to Kuwaiti youth to encourage them to start their own businesses, take risks, and step out of their safety zones. They talked about the need to learn from failure and mistakes and that they should not be afraid of experiencing either. Failure is not something to feel stigmatized by, but rather something to embrace and learn from in order to do better next time. In a society where failure can bring shame to the individual as well as his or her entire family, this was an important message to deliver.

LOYAC, another organization founded to support youth in Kuwait, has been so successful that it expanded its presence into other Middle Eastern countries. This organization is run by a small group of committed Kuwaiti women who, following the September 11 terrorist attack against the United States, recognized that idle youth were susceptible to being radicalized, especially if there were no opportunities available to help them be productive members of society. The women founded LOYAC to provide youth with opportunities to grow, volunteer, and develop professional skills. LOYAC provides opportunities in the Kuwaiti business community and public sector by establishing internships, training programs, and volunteer projects for youth throughout the year.

One of the founding members invited me to the opening of the 2015 summer LOYAC program for youth. At the opening ceremony, she put up a slide in English as she addressed the audience in Arabic. The slide projected behind her read, "Today I am not going to give you a speech. Today I am going to tell you a story... a story about success. It all started in 2002 under very similar circumstances that we are having recently in our Arab world, where terrorism is trying to spread all over the Arab countries until they reached our beloved Kuwait, the center of safety and security." It was her way of reminding people that the dangers of radicalism were not far, especially in view of the 2014 takeover of large swaths of land by ISIS terrorists in nearby Iraq and Syria. Keeping youth in Kuwait safe from the reach of radicals was paramount, at least from what I could glean from her slide.

The gathering celebrated the start of some 850 internships for young people throughout Kuwait. The internships were not limited to Kuwaiti youth but also were extended to the sons and daughters of the many expatriates that raise their families in Kuwait. Many of these expatriate families are far less advantaged than the Kuwaitis and also need to have opportunities for their children so they too grow and lead productive lives. I was impressed that LOYAC recognized the fact that three-quarters of Kuwait's population was comprised of expatriates.

Expat laborers often lead difficult lives in Kuwait. Foreigners who come to work in Kuwait are sponsored by a Kuwaiti citizen or company known as a *kafeel*, or "sponsor" in English. The *kafala* system, which similarly operates in other countries in the Gulf, gives private Kuwaiti citizens and companies a great deal of authority over foreign laborers they wish to bring into the country. For years, there was little oversight as to how foreign laborers were treated once they arrived. Not surprisingly, there has been a lot of abuse.

Domestic workers living in people's homes are particularly vulnerable, and incidents of violence, sexual abuse, and overwork have been the result. There have also been instances in which domestic workers have exacted their vengeance upon their Kuwaiti sponsors. In February 2016, for example, a 23-year old Kuwaiti woman was brutally murdered while she slept, allegedly by the foreign domestic servant employed by her family.[cxliii] Despite these unseemly episodes, working in the Gulf has been an enormous economic opportunity for an untold number of foreign laborers and families around the world have benefited.

Foreign laborers and professionals began arriving in Kuwait with the oil boom. They came to run the grocery stores, build the roads, work in the hospitals, teach in the schools, and help administer the vast amount of wealth pouring into the country. There simply were not enough Kuwaitis to do these jobs and so the country would never again be just for Kuwaitis. I have met a number of families of Persian, Syrian, Iraqi, Egyptian, and Palestinian backgrounds who were lucky enough to become Kuwaiti citizens in recognition of their ancestors' contributions to the country. But the vast majority of guest workers live today without citizenship status. These newer arrivals focus on the fact they are gainfully employed and less on the fact they have no political rights. While many guest workers can afford to marry, and raise their families in Kuwait, most live in low rent squalor, sending money back home to loved ones whom they cannot afford to support here. Even for the wealthy guest workers, the lifestyle has its drawbacks. A successful Egyptian executive told me he was thinking of moving to Canada, because his children have come to believe they are "Kuwaiti" since they have grown up in the country. He and his wife did not have the heart to explain they were not. Though his children held Egyptian passports, they had no idea about what it meant to be "Egyptian", nor did their parents necessarily want their children to live in Egypt with all its problems today. Canada seemed the best option for now.

To Kuwait's credit, I have heard offspring of expatriate families raised in Kuwait say they are loyal to the country and love Kuwait as their home. Some of these expatriates, born and raised in Kuwait, work at the U.S. embassy. Their salaries are not very high, at least not high enough for Kuwaiti citizens, but they have relatively good jobs compared to what many expats find on the local economy. One U.S. embassy expat employee told me once that she felt more "Kuwaiti" than the Syrian nationality of her parents. She was content to accept that she would never share in the country's welfare benefits in return for the peace and stability Kuwait offered.

Although the *kafala* system in Kuwait has been significantly reformed through new labor and domestic labor laws, reports of abuse continue.[cxliv] Many end up working for years in Kuwait before they earn enough to go home. When I went to the home of a Filipina guest worker recommended to me as an excellent seamstress, I learned this firsthand. She had come to Kuwait 10 years before, following her childhood dream to become a tailor and was now employed in a Kuwaiti dress shop. As I entered her apartment building, I was shocked by what I saw. I could hardly breath from the smell of urine in the stairwell. The hall was dark and damp as the tenants took care to keep their energy bills low. Even though energy is cheap, they preferred to save money wherever they could. Her room must have been no more than eight by 10 feet. There was no sunlight because the room had been boarded up to divide the space with other renters. Somehow, she managed to fit a sewing machine, chair, bed, and a small dresser with a mirror into the room, making it very difficult to walk and turn around. There was a small closet covered with a curtain and a TV hung on the wall over her bed.

She told me she paid 50 KD (just over $165.00) a month to live alone in her small room along with several other tenants who shared the larger apartment together.[cxlv] I could not determine how many were living in the apartment, but I suspected that if at least five other women were living in their own small rooms, the landlord was probably making about a $1,000 a month, more if additional women were crammed into the apartment. There were also plenty of other apartments in the building, most likely in similar crowded conditions in order to get the highest rent from people making the lowest salaries. Many Kuwaitis have become very wealthy renting out accommodations to expat laborers since current law forbids non-citizens to own their own real estate in Kuwait.[cxlvi] This was another example of how the economy of non-Kuwaitis living in the country was so vastly different from the economy enjoyed by those who hold citizenship.

# CHAPTER FIFTEEN

## *Perils of Wealth*

Imagine you are in a country the size of New Jersey wedged between heavyweights like Iran, Iraq and Saudi Arabia. Your national citizenry is only over a million people but you are blessed with incredible wealth from the discovery of oil. What would you do? You probably would do what the Kuwaitis have been doing since their independence in 1961: work hard to maintain excellent relations with countries around the world and provide generous financial assistance to secure their goodwill. I have never served in a country where there are so many diplomatic missions present. It is possible to attend a diplomatic function in Kuwait almost every night of the year. I am constantly meeting ambassadors and their spouses from across the globe, as far away as Peru and Cuba, Vietnam and Bhutan, Swaziland and Burkina Faso. Kuwait knows the importance of having international friends, especially when it comes to threats to its national security. The strong support Kuwait received in the United Nations Security Council against Iraq's invasion of Kuwait on August 2, 1990 helped secure Kuwait's ultimate liberation.

In addition to deepening relations around the world, Kuwait offers robust assistance abroad. It has been consistently generous in providing financial aid to victims of natural disasters, war, political unrest and instability since its independence in 1961. These years of generosity culminated on September 8, 2014 when UN Secretary General Ban Ki-moon recognized Kuwait's leader Amir Sheikh Sabah Al-Ahmed at an official ceremony in New York as Humanitarian Leader. This was a true honor for Kuwait and the way Kuwaitis want to be seen in the world.

In 1961 the late Amir, Sheikh Jaber Al-Ahmad Al-Jabber Al-Sabah, then Minister of Finance, had the foresight to establish the Kuwait Fund for Arab Economic Development, the first aid agency in the world to be established by a developing country. In 1967, as Prime Minister, Sheikh Jabber also supported Kuwait taking the lead to establish the regional organization known as the Arab Fund for Social and Economic Development. Today the Arab Fund's 21 members support key projects in the Arab world that seek to improve education, electricity, transportation and communications as well as reduce poverty and improve social services.

In recognition of Kuwait's leadership role, the Arab Fund made its headquarters inside the beautiful Arab Organizations Headquarters Building located in Kuwait. The building, completed in 1994, is an awe-inspiring symbol of the great wealth of the oil rich Arab nations. I have taken several visitors to the Arab Headquarters Building. Each time I find the classical Islamic and contemporary arabesque designs more breathtaking. Damascene fountains, Jordanian stonework, Moroccan brass chandeliers, Egyptian carved wood, Tunisian tiles, and Iraqi paintings showcase the Arab world's mesmerizing sense of style and symmetry. It is a landmark for all to see when visiting Kuwait and a monument to Kuwait's giving.

In keeping with its charitable giving, Kuwait has been laser-focused on the humanitarian crisis in Syria since it began in 2011. The Kuwaiti government has been a steady and reliable donor to Syrian refugees. In addition to hosting three consecutive major donor conferences for Syria, Kuwait has hosted smaller quarterly conferences among the key international donor states and the key international aid organizations to decide how best to spend that money. I accompanied Doug to attend one of these quarterly coordination conferences early in October 2014 and was extremely impressed by the level of priority the most senior Kuwaiti officials gave to this effort. Various donor countries sent their representatives to announce at the meeting how much aid they intended to give. Kuwait, however, has kept the bar high.

Later, on March 31, 2015, Kuwait hosted the Third Syria Major Donors conference at the Amir's Bayan Palace and according to local press reports, donors pledged almost four billion dollars to assist the Syrian refugees. Just prior to the conference, Amir Sabah Al-Ahmed pledged $500 million dollars while the United States, represented by then-U.S. Ambassador to the United Nations Samantha Power, pledged $507 million. The rest came from other European, Arab and Asian donor nations at the conference. Between 2013 and 2016, the State of Kuwait alone provided well over one billion dollars to help the Syrian refugees. In the aid community, Kuwait holds a special place because it is known for making good on its promises and actually writing the checks.

Kuwait, however, has not opened its borders to refugees. Kuwait is not required to do so by international law as it is not a signatory of the U.N.'s 1951 Convention relating to the Status of Refugees. Geographically far, it is difficult for large numbers of Syrian refugees to arrive to Kuwait over land. Migration through Iraq and Saudi Arabia has also been prohibitive. Summer temperatures, often well over 100 degrees, would be physically exhausting for migrants. It will be interesting to see, however, if there is any future pressure on Kuwait to open its doors to at least some Syrian refugees. While there has been no call for this locally, international media have certainly raised the idea. Given the country's strict visa requirements and complex labor laws, accepting a flow of refugees is not something that is likely to happen in the near future. For the time being, the Kuwaitis are happy to open their pocketbooks instead.

They are also happy to open their hearts. Dr. Hilal Al-Sayer, the Deputy President of the Kuwait Red Crescent Society, Board Chairman of Dasman Diabetes Institute, and Board Chairman of the Bayt Abdullah Children's Hospital, travels often to visit Syrian refugees in Lebanon and Jordan to provide funding directly to those in need. At a dinner in March 2016, he told me he had recently met a little Syrian refugee in Jordan who was on a dialysis machine.[cxlvii] He noticed she was not smiling at all and so he asked her why. She said she did not like having to be on this scary machine at least four hours every week. Her mother and father told Dr. Al-Sayer both of them would donate a kidney to her but that they could not afford the operation. Dr. Al-Sayer immediately made plans to pay for it, as he became quite attached to this little girl.[cxlviii] A photograph of him holding the little Syrian girl following the operation went viral in Kuwait and was displayed as part of a light show on top of the famous Kuwait Towers. They both had big smiles as he held her close with joy. Kuwait's generosity transcends the region. Ten years ago, the Kuwait Red Crescent Society donated $30 million to the American Red Cross in response to Hurricane Katrina; Dr. Al-Sayer personally went to Washington, D.C. to hand over the check.[cxlix]

There is a dark side to financial support from the Gulf, however, that perhaps unwittingly, may have helped fuel the horrible demise of the once lovely country of Syria. The people of the region have a deep sympathy for the Syrian people and their country. I can understand why. I travelled in Syria extensively as a tourist and lived there for the summer of 1986 to work temporarily at the U.S. embassy in Damascus. The Syrian people I met were kind and hardworking. As a secular and socialist state, the people were guaranteed an education, including attendance at university. Syrian women could be seen both in the universities and in the workplace; they were participating fully in the economic life of the country. I remember in particular the wonderful Syrian women who worked at our U.S. embassy there.

Looking back on my summer in Syria, it is very sad to see this beautiful country so destroyed but I also had known the sectarian strife was well underway, just brutally stifled for decades. I remember arriving only a few years after President Hafiz al-Asad, Bashar's father, launched a deadly attack on the Sunni Muslim stronghold in Hama in 1981–82. Thousands were killed. Back then, the elder Asad's security men were posted on practically every street corner in Damascus as if not to let anyone forget who was in charge. They wore tailored double-breasted suit jackets and carried AK-47 assault rifles. I did my best to avoid them whenever I walked between the embassy and my apartment. Everywhere in Damascus there was fear of the Asad regime and its omnipresence. When people asked me in the States how my summer in Damascus was, I would say, "Well, I still have my fingernails." I must have been channeling the fear and oppression I sensed while there. Pulling fingernails was a catchall phrase for the random forms of persecution suffered by the regime's many opponents if held by Asad's security services.

But I really enjoyed my summer in Syria. The country was beautiful. The hospitality and cuisine were sensational. To this day, my favorite Syrian dish is *muhammara*, the delicious roasted red pepper dip made with ground walnuts and pomegranate syrup. I have fond memories of savoring it on a table spread full of other tasty dishes similar to those found in Lebanon and Turkey. I delighted in going to the countryside just outside Damascus to the lovely outdoor restaurants of Bludan. Over long lunches, it was wonderful to see the mountain forests and hear the fresh water springs. It was equally enjoyable to eat at the restaurants in the city. One restaurant in particular served delicious caviar and vodka, neither of which I had ever tasted before. These were of the highest quality and I remember being able to afford them easily. The prices were reasonable due to the large presence of Soviets in the country at the time. I found the massive Soviet embassy compound astonishing compared to the rather small townhouse where our U.S. embassy once stood before it was evacuated due to the crisis.

The *suq* (market) in the Old City was unparalleled. Its embroidered tablecloths, hand-woven carpets, and filigreed gold and silver jewelry were always arranged in alluring displays in shop after shop. My favorite stalls along the main corridor of the *suq* were the ones filled with colorful and provocative women's lingerie. I had never seen such fetching underwear and the sight of women in long black robes carefully selecting from the piles caught me by surprise each time. Of course, now I understand that covering in public does not mean that you must be modest in your personal life at home. On the contrary, I am told!

Further into the *suq* is the incredible Umayyad Mosque, one of the oldest and most revered mosques. The sixth Caliph of the Umayyad Dynasty commissioned the construction of the mosque in 706 AD. The site of the mosque is actually where a Christian basilica built during the Byzantine era once stood. Before that, it was the site of a grand Roman temple dedicated to Jupiter.[cl] Not surprising, Damascus is often referred to as one of the oldest continuously inhabited cities in the world. The last time I was in Damascus was in the early 2000's while we were living in Jordan when my husband was serving as the Political Counselor at the U.S. embassy in Amman. Only a few hours away, it was fairly easy to drive to Damascus for a weekend visit. By then, the trend in Damascus was for private businesses to renovate the older buildings in the Old City into lavish boutique restaurants and hotels. These were extremely nice places to eat and spend the night. I did notice, however, that the Syrian government had done little to preserve the outer walls of the Old City or the rest of the common areas since the time I had been there in the mid-1980's. I was saddened to see that the Old City looked worse than I had remembered.

Visiting some of the beautiful Christian sites like the Byzantine monastery of Saidnaya outside of Damascus and the churches of the Christian Assyrian people were a very moving experiences. I understand these Christian communities have since either managed to depart Syria or have been savagely threatened by the presence of Islamic State of Iraq and Syria (ISIS). I also had the opportunity to see the amazing ruins of Palmyra in central Syria, an ancient city that became by the 3rd century AD a metropolis at the crossroads of east-west trade. It will be a great travesty if these ruins are lost to ISIS destruction.

In the 1800's Palmyra was a favorite destination for adventurous British aristocrats to experience a romantic trek across the desert. Among the most famous of these wealthy British tourists was Jane Digby, also known as Lady Ellenborough, who fell in love with a Bedouin sheikh who was her guide to the ancient city of Palmyra.[cli] I discovered her in a magnificent portrait of her exhibited at the Tareq Rajab Museum in Kuwait. I was compelled to learn more about her story of multiple marriages to and divorces from aristocrats across Europe before finding her ultimate happiness in the Middle East.

Still a beauty in her fifties by the time she arrived in Damascus in the 1850's, Jane Digby married Syrian Sheikh Medjuel El-Mezrab and lived her remaining years immersed in the Bedouin way of life. Her letters recall constant raids or *ghazu* that were integral to the desert culture of Syria. These raids would often force her to leave the desert where she genuinely loved living with the Bedouin women, learning their desert culture and helping to care for their animals. She was an amazing horseback rider and she knew how to tend a garden as well as care for animals. These skills, in addition to her confidence and independence uncharacteristic of her Victorian England, helped Digby earn the respect of the local tribes.[clii] I wonder if Jane Digby didn't turn in her grave at the thought of ISIS's raid on her beloved Palmyra.

The tragedy of the Syrian crisis has moved us all in one way or another and I like many people have wanted to help. When I suggested that I would like to get involved in helping the refugees when we arrived in Kuwait in 2014, my husband admonished that this would not be a good idea for the wife of the American ambassador. Certain private citizens in Kuwait, I would later learn, were involved in funding illicit groups in the Syrian campaign to oust the Asad government, some of whom the U.S. Government had officially named as terrorists. It would be problematic for an American associated with our embassy to be involved in charity work that might support the wrong people.

Eventually a wonderful opportunity came up that would allow me to help the Syrian refugees. A student group at Kuwait's Gulf University for Science and Technology (GUST) arranged a huge clothing drive where I only needed to drive up to a parking lot and drop off a few loads of used clothing. No money would change hands. It was winter and my cold weather clothes would be greatly appreciated by the Syrian refugees in Lebanon, Syria and Jordan. To my delight, the clothing drive took on a much greater dimension. Suddenly the goal was not only to help the refugees but also to beat Qatar where students had collected 29 tons of clothing the previous year. With the help of social media spurring people to beat Qatar, on January 31, 2015, Kuwait proudly announced it had collected over 56 tons of clothes for the Syrian refugees in 24 hours.[cliii]

There is great national pride in charitable giving here in Kuwait. But, unfortunately some of the charitable giving from Kuwait that occurred early on in the Syria crisis stoked the fires of the crisis rather than tamped them down. I raise this blight on Kuwait's otherwise magnanimous role in the Syrian humanitarian crisis because it is worth drawing attention to how money from wealthy private donors may have inadvertently helped to prolong the conflict and make it so terribly lethal.

Follow the money and you will see an awful lot of wealth in the Gulf. It should not be surprising that there are people with deep pockets in the region whose political agendas may not match those of their government or the U.S. Back in

2011, there were those in Kuwait who were also motivated to oust Asad, an Alawite, and his secular, socialist brand of government and establish Sunni Islamic rule in Syria. These early benefactors from the Gulf were also angered by Bashar al-Asad's heavy hand against the political protests of Syria's Arab Spring in 2011. Sunni Muslims, a majority of Syria's population, demanded Bashar Asad's ouster much the way the Arab Spring in Cairo called for Egyptian President Husni Mubarak to step down. What these protesters were not prepared for was the swiftness and ruthlessness of Asad's response and his unwillingness to compromise. To do so, in Asad's mind, would threaten the very survival of his family, his minority Alawite community, as well as the entrenched, corrupt socialist government from which some Sunni families also benefit.

Meanwhile in Kuwait, the early unrest in Syria was closely felt by the presence of more than 100,000 Syrian expatriates living and working in Kuwait for decades. Over the years the Syrian expat community developed close relationships with their Kuwaiti employers. The Syrians, unlike many of the Asian migrants in Kuwait, shared a common language and culture. These Syrian guest workers tended to be more educated and were largely members of the professional class in Kuwait. Each Syrian expat in Kuwait had his or her own story to tell, including a special village to call home or a distinctive tribe to declare family. While they hailed from different social backgrounds, these Syrian expats for the most part shared a common bond in that they were not among the beneficiaries of the Syrian government structure. Although they agreed the Asad regime should go, they did not share a common vision of what a new Syrian government should be.

The Syrian expat community residing in Kuwait quickly succeeded in persuading their Kuwaiti patrons to support their individual causes back home to ensure their loved ones would be supported and protected. Elizabeth Dickinson, in her research for the Brookings Institute entitled *"Playing with Fire: Why Private Gulf Financing for Syria's Extremists Rebels Risks*

*Igniting Sectarian Conflict at Home,*" captured the relative ease with which funds were raised in Kuwait and flowed to Syria.[cliv] Her work described in detail how Syrians in Kuwait approached Kuwaiti charities and individual Kuwaiti donors and how the Kuwaitis would rely on their individual Syrian contacts to get the money to Syria. Suddenly hundreds of individual income streams were flowing from Kuwait to Syria. As the Asad government committed more and more atrocities against the Syrian people, some Kuwaiti charities and donors began turning their humanitarian assistance into sending arms. Thus began, according to Dickinson, the rise of hundreds of rebel brigades, each with their individual Kuwaiti financier and each relying on its own steady flow of income. Of course, Kuwait was not the only source of income on the Arabian Peninsula. Other wealthy oil nationals were similarly involved.

The conflict continued to heat up while Syrian expats broadened their fundraising efforts by attending the various Kuwaiti *diwaniyyas* and Friday services in the local mosques. They soon convinced their Kuwaiti supporters to use social media and popular cell phone apps like *WhatsApp* to raise funds. Dickinson described a particularly brazen effort known as the *Ramadan Campaign* to raise funds in 2011. Nineteen Kuwaiti clerics, politicians, and public figures, according to Dickinson, participated in fundraising efforts "to prepare 12,000 jihadists for the sake of Allah." One campaign poster promised that a donation of 700 KD (about $2,300) would prepare a single fighter for battle.[clv]

As of 2011, Kuwait had not yet criminalized terrorist financing. There was no established national Financial Intelligence Unit or implementation of the relevant UN terrorist financing conventions and resolutions. In other words, there was little effort to control or censor those in Kuwait involved in funding the Syrian humanitarian crisis or the armed Syrian opposition forces. It was not long until private Kuwaitis found themselves funding Syrian opposition forces aligned with groups that opposed each other, and it was difficult to know who was moderate and who was not.

Extremists had entered the fray, including ISIS. By then the chance for moderate groups to unite against the Syrian government had disappeared. Instead, there was chaos, and the situation grew worse and more violent; Syria became a prolonged and debilitating crisis, and the exodus of refugees from Syria put Europe and the rest of the world on edge. By 2014, the international community had to put a stop to the flow of money supporting this internal conflict.

A few months before we arrived in Kuwait in summer 2014, then U.S. Treasury Undersecretary for Terrorism and Financial Intelligence David Cohen publicly described Kuwait as "the epicenter of fundraising for terrorist groups in Syria." This was a rather harsh statement but it did get the required attention. The last thing Kuwait wanted was to be in any way associated with terrorism. After considerable pressure from the U.S. government and others, the Kuwaiti Parliament passed the Counterterrorism Finance Law in 2014 and began working with the International Monetary Fund to set up a Financial Intelligence Unit. These actions now regulate charities more closely and prohibit unlicensed groups from collecting money. This has helped stem the flow of private funds from Kuwait to Syria, and there are no longer public campaigns to raise funds to arm the opposition.

This is not to say that the funding of extremists and terrorists in Syria is no longer happening in Kuwait. The flow of money has likely just gone underground, but Kuwait has made it undeniably harder for illicit fundraising to be done in public. For me, Dickinson's research pointed to the inconvenient truth that there were those in Kuwait who probably supported extremism, who were interested in establishing an Islamic form of government in Syria and elsewhere, and possibly even in their own country. Thus, Kuwait, at least when we arrived in 2014, was hardly free from the pressures of radicalism that had grown exponentially in the region with the rise of ISIS.

# CHAPTER SIXTEEN

## *The Terror Next Door*

It was 6:52 am on November 10, 2014, only a couple of months after I had arrived in Kuwait. Sirens began to ring out on the U.S. embassy compound where the ambassador's residence is located. An electronic voice wailed repeatedly for everyone to go into his or her safe haven. Then the order "Duck and cover! Get away from the windows!" was commanded over and over via the Embassy loudspeakers. We were usually up by 5:30 am to get our son Zach off to school, and so Doug and I moved quickly from our small breakfast table to our safe haven. First, we managed to get our confused elderly Bernese Mountain dog up to join us. I was glad our son had already left the compound on his school bus.

Having just arrived in Kuwait, I was scared and lay on the floor next to our dog not really knowing what was happening. Was there a bomb planted on the compound? I knew the previous U.S. embassy in Kuwait that was once located near the sea had been seriously bombed in 1983. My mind then dwelled on our last post in Ankara, Turkey. I was thinking how I felt so safe there but then the back gate of our embassy in Ankara -- the gate my family used regularly -- was bombed in 2013, a year after we departed post. Had I once again allowed myself to be lulled into thinking everything was safe when it really was not?

When I finally noticed my husband, he was looking rather relaxed. "Now you know what it is like to be at our embassy in Baghdad," was all he said. Great, I thought. He had grown used to these sirens when the U.S. embassy in Iraq was taking regular 107 mm rocket hits just prior to the U.S. withdrawal of troops in 2011. Within a few minutes, one of the U.S. Marine Guards got on the speaker and gave the "all clear". A foreign visa applicant had unwittingly veered his car outside the lane to enter the compound and the embassy guard, not sure what this guy was trying to do, sounded the alarm.

There is no margin for error in the security of our Embassies overseas. I am reminded of this daily because I live in a fortress. To exit the compound of the U.S. embassy, security guards raise drop bars and lower gate barriers and only then am I able to drive through the obstacle course of carefully placed roadblocks. To get back into the embassy I must go through checkpoints and car inspections. I have had to put aside my desire to get to and from where I want to go quickly. I have come to accept the rigorous security arrangements as part of my life. This comes with the territory of being a member of the official American community overseas. In the aftermath of Ambassador Chris Stevens' murder in Benghazi, Libya, on September 12, 2012, security operations are under the spotlight and therefore even stricter. My husband is not allowed to set foot outside the compound without a full security detail. That means no quiet walks along the beach or romantic dinners overlooking the sea without the company of a noticeable number of security personnel from the Kuwaiti Interior Ministry. Believe me, this part of the job is not easy for either one of us.

Lessons from the past pointed to the need for the U.S. embassy in Kuwait to be located inside a highly protected compound. On December 12, 1983, two men crashed a dump truck packed with explosives through the gate of the original U.S. embassy compound that once stood not far from the sea near the famous Kuwait Towers. The bomb exploded next to the U.S. Consulate building, destroying it and heavily damaging the Chancery. Three foreigners who worked for the embassy were killed and no Americans. One of the foreigners was engaged to an American woman who continues to live and work in Kuwait to this day. I met her at an American Women's League event. She made a point to tell me that every year on December 12, she sends flowers to the U.S. embassy compound to be placed at a special memorial dedicated to her fiancé and the other two men who lost their lives that day. I probably would not have known what this interesting sculpture was all about set amidst a row of palm trees along the entrance of the embassy if she had not told me. History and lives can be forgotten without the help of people who keep memories alive.

A Shi'a group known as Al-Dawa, or "the Call", carried out the bombing. Among the 17 people -- infamously known at the time as *the Kuwait 17* -- arrested and convicted was Moustafa Youssef Badreddin, a cousin and brother-in-law of Imad Mughniyah. Mughniyah in the 1980's was the renowned terrorist mastermind for the Iran-backed Lebanese Hezbollah involved in numerous bombings, assassinations, and hijackings in Lebanon and elsewhere. Most notably, Mughniyah was behind the harrowing kidnappings of several U.S. and other western hostages living in Lebanon during the 1980's. The actions of these hardcore Shi'a radicals not long after the Islamic revolution in Iran are not forgotten in Kuwait.

By 1990, Saddam Hussein's invasion of Kuwait tested U.S. embassy security on an unimaginable scale. While the 1980's consumed the U.S. embassy's focus on Iranian-backed terrorist attacks, the embassy suddenly found itself surrounded by invading Iraqi military forces. This did not deter then-U.S. Ambassador W. Nathaniel Howell III though. He decided to defy Saddam's orders to vacate the embassy and instead remained for 110 days, operating in the makeshift trailers that constituted the embassy as a result of the 1983 bombing. Howell was determined to stay until all American citizens were able to leave Kuwait safely.[clvi] Eventually, those Americans who wanted to leave, were able to evacuate and embassy staff decided to leave themselves. During those four months, however, staff inside the U.S. compound managed without city power and tap water. They were very brave to stay, literally surrounded by hostile troops and forced to survive on internal stocks and the few supplies the Iraqis permitted them.

After Kuwait's liberation from Iraq by a multinational force under the command of U.S. Army General Norman Schwarzkopf in 1991, the U.S. embassy was eventually moved from its prime real estate location on the sea to the very large and secure compound next to the Amir's Palace in the neighborhood of Bayan. The new compound was provided as a gesture of great appreciation from the Kuwaiti government. Today the U.S. embassy is far from the congestion of downtown and enjoys relative peace and quiet, lulling residents into believing they live in a very serene and peaceful place.

Compounding this sense of serenity are the parts of Kuwait City that appear like Hollywood sets on a desert location with extravagant yachts, opulent villas, and over-the-top malls. But when you consider geographically where you are located, you crash pretty quickly to reality. Living so close to nations that support terror or are overwhelmed by terrorists, was on the minds of everyone in Kuwait. It may not have been the number one topic of conversation in 2014, but it was not far from people's thoughts. Needless to say, when sirens go off at the U.S. Embassy in Kuwait, you simply had to take it very seriously.

While I was living in Kuwait, when something went wrong in the country, the first thing people thought was that DA'ISH was behind it. DA'ISH is the acronym for *Al-Dawlah Al-Islamiyah fi Al-Iraq wa Al-Sham*. In English, the group is referred to as the Islamic State in Iraq and Syria (ISIS). Whatever the name, it was frightening that this Sunni extremist brand sought totalitarian rule of the region and the establishment of a Caliphate. For Kuwait, Sunni extremism had become a serious concern.

Fear of ISIS was palpable in Kuwait when we first arrived in 2014, particularly since the group's leader, Abu Bakr Al-Baghdadi, had succeeded in taking large swaths of territory for its evil caliphate in Iraq, including Iraq's second largest city of Mosul. So, when Kuwait experienced a massive power outage due to a technical failure at one of the major power grids one evening in February 2015, almost reflexively, Kuwaitis believed ISIS was somehow behind it. It was as if Kuwaitis half expected to be overrun by this terror group overnight. One of my instructors at the gym I attended, a tall and independent young Egyptian woman, told me the next day she had been terrified driving home alone that night. The lights were completely out and it was pitch black on the roads. She half expected an ISIS terrorist to jump in her car and take her away. An American friend married to a Kuwaiti texted me that night saying she and others were convinced ISIS was behind the power outage.

This aversion to ISIS was borne out in an October 2015 poll sponsored by the Washington Institute for Near East Policy of 1,000 random adult Kuwaiti nationals. A full 92 percent of Kuwaitis had a very negative opinion of ISIS and viewed the group as the number one national security issue for Kuwait. So, it was not surprising then for me to hear personally the prevalence of fear in Kuwait toward falling victim to ISIS terror. I recall a Syrian-American friend who grew up in Kuwait but decided to return to the United States in May 2015, confiding she was certain there was going to be trouble in Kuwait. Something could easily happen in Kuwait, she warned, as her departure date drew near.

She was not far from the truth in her foreboding when a bomb blasted inside the crowded Shi'a Imam Al-Sadiq Mosque in downtown Kuwait the following month on June 26, 2015. The attack killed 27 people and wounded more than 200 worshippers. The explosion occurred during Friday prayers in a mosque packed with 2,000 worshippers.[clvii] It came less than 10 days into the holy month of Ramadan.

ISIS quickly claimed responsibility for the bombing in a posting on Twitter and identified the suicide-bomber as a Saudi man who blew himself up with the explosives vest he was wearing. Authorities would later name the bomber as 23-year-old Fahd Suleiman Abdulmohsen al-Qaba'a who had flown from Saudi Arabia via Bahrain. He had arrived in Kuwait early that Friday morning on June 26. Kuwaiti authorities later picked up the man who drove the bomber from the airport to the mosque. He was a *bidoon* from Kuwait.

*Bidoon* is the Arabic term that describes a group of people in Kuwait who are stateless, who are *without nationality*. There are over 100,000 *bidoon* in Kuwait.[clviii] They live on the margins of society with little access to public assistance, including education, as they do not qualify because they do not have the Kuwaiti citizenship. Most Kuwaitis have come to see *bidoon* as merely illegal guest workers who already have another nationality from neighboring Iraq, Saudi Arabia, or Iran, but who are instead trying to claim Kuwaiti citizenship in order to obtain the welfare benefits. Whatever the case, this group of people in Kuwait is certainly fertile ground for extremism.

The driver, whose name is 'Abdulrahman Sabah Saud, was only 26 years old at the time of the bombing. Both he and the Saudi youth are two of an untold number of Muslim youth who have fallen prey to the lure of ISIS and its extremist beliefs. Somewhere, both youth received educations distorted by Sunni extremist religious ideologies and became compelled to carry out the extremist doctrines they learned, doctrines filled with hatred and intolerance. Worse, they swore allegiance to follow their leader, the Caliph of the Islamic State, even if he tells them to kill. They were not unlike the radicalized couple in San Bernadino, California, Tashfeen Malik and Syed Farook, who killed 14 and injured dozens of Americans on December 2, 2015, at a health department gathering for training employees and celebrating the Christmas season.

When the terrorists targeted the Shi'a mosque in Kuwait at the direction of an ISIS affiliate from Saudi Arabia known as *The Islamic State of Najd Province*, their goal was to undermine the peaceful and tolerant society that Kuwait is known to uphold.[clix] In Kuwait, there may be as many as 30 percent of the population belonging to the Shi'a sect, with the remaining being Sunni Muslims. Tolerance and respect for both sects of the religion are crucial to Kuwait's survival, as extremism and sectarianism would almost certainly lead to its demise. Thus, the stakes are very high for Kuwait to remain above all forms of bigotry and hate. Kuwaitis understand this and know they must work together to ensure peace and stability.

This is one of many reasons why ISIS and its brand of Sunni extremism have been largely rejected in Kuwait. The majority Sunni population in Kuwait simply does not support ISIS radicals who condemn fellow Muslim Shi'ites, whom ISIS labels as *"the followers of 'Ali,"* as infidels. There are many differences between the Sunni and Shi'a branches of Islam, and for the majority of Muslims they are not worth fighting over. Sunnis and Shiites essentially differ in how they perceive the Prophet Mohammad. Sunnis follow the sayings and deeds of the Prophet Mohammad and believe he was a human being to whom God revealed his message in the Quran. Shiites, on the other hand, contend that the Prophet was infallible and possessed semi-divine attributes of all of God's prophets.[clx]

Shi'a mourn the slaying of the prophet's grandson Hussein when he tried to reclaim the caliphate from the Umayyads at the Battle of Karbala. Although the Umayyads came from Mecca, they were not blood members of the Prophet's family, and this remains a key dividing point between Shi'a and Sunni. To this day, Shi'a Muslims commemorate the Prophet's grandson, Imam Hussain, and his martyrdom, through recitations, processions, and passion plays that memorialize his story. During the month of Ramadan, his story is retold and retold each evening in a gathering known as a *kraya.*[clxi]

Recognition of who were the first four Caliphs of Islam, how they derive and render Islamic jurisprudence, their chosen rituals and how they practice liturgical prayers appear to be the main causes for division among Muslims.<sup>clxii</sup> Unfortunately, extremists on both sides have chosen to fight and kill over their religious divergences. Although many of us, including Muslims, may view fighting over religious differences as pointless, sectarianism has nonetheless become a very dangerous and destabilizing reality in the 21st century. Much of the violence we see in Muslim majority countries like Iraq, Syria, Yemen, Pakistan, and Afghanistan has its roots in 7th century Sunni-Shi'a rivalries.

No one in Kuwait understood the threat to incite sectarianism better than the Amir of Kuwait, Sheikh Sabah Al-Ahmed. As soon as he heard about the bombing at the Imam Sadiq Mosque, he rushed to the scene, arriving within minutes of the attack. The Amir, in his mid-eighties, was determined to reassure his people. He needed to show that the country could withstand this attack and above all, not let it lead to counterattacks. Upon seeing the victims in the destroyed mosque that day, he said immediately what he felt. "These are my people." His words spread like wildfire, heard again and again on Instagram videos and Twitter retweets. The country united. Kuwaitis stood shoulder-to-shoulder, Shi'a and Sunni, vowing not to let the attack tear them apart. Kuwait became on that day the role model of how respect and tolerance could win over the evils of intolerance and bigotry.<sup>clxiii</sup>

Following the bombing, in accordance with Islamic law, the dead were buried within 24 hours. A three-day *'aza'*, or condolence call, was then immediately arranged for the 27 families who lost their loved ones in the bombing. At the *'aza'* for women, I recognized some of the ladies who had lost loved ones or who had someone inside the mosque during the bombing. When I went to offer my condolences at the large public hall, I saw an acquaintance standing in line behind me. I met her at a U.S. embassy public affairs event for Kuwaitis who had participated in U.S. government leadership and professional exchange programs. I was surprised to see her in her black *abbaya*; she normally dressed in such vivid colors. I had been following her on Instagram and that was how I thought of her. I was shocked when she told me her father was in the hospital from the bombing. Her family's Indian driver had died in the explosion. I was stunned and felt so sad for her and her grieving family standing in line with her. I did not realize that she was Shi'a. In Kuwait, it is not the first thing you learn about people when you meet them. It is not something that seems to matter a great deal, though Kuwaitis know often by the name who is Shi'a and who is Sunni.

Later, I learned that the husband of one of my favorite couples in Kuwait was actually inside the mosque during the bombing. I had grown accustomed to seeing both on the Kuwaiti social scene. When the bomb exploded on June 26, 2015, however, she was abroad awaiting the arrival of their grandchild. He had found time during the holy month of Ramadan to pray. He chose not to talk about the horror he witnessed seeing 27 people die on that fateful day.

It was an incredibly moving experience to grieve at the *'aza'* with the women who had just lost their loved ones. Out of respect, I covered my hair with my shawl and proceeded to hug each woman. The kisses and hugs I received back were overwhelming. The women were of all ages. They were mothers, sisters, daughters, and wives. They all wore black *abayyas* and hijabs; their eyes were full of tears. There was so much sadness in the room. How many times have I heard about attacks on Shi'a mosques in the past? But this was the first time I saw the devastation personally. Attending as the wife of the American ambassador, I also felt a huge weight I had not felt before. Suddenly I felt the power of our nation and how all these women were looking to the United States to keep them safe and secure. I found myself assuring each woman that the United States was with Kuwait and would keep her family and country safe. It came so naturally because this was what they needed to hear.

Meanwhile my husband attended the *'aza'* for men held in the Grand Mosque. He went on the first day that also happened to coincide with a visit to Kuwait of a U.S. congressional delegation. The group was heading to our embassy in Baghdad but Doug thought it would be extremely important if the congressmen and woman could personally offer their condolences as well. They all managed to express their condolences to the families of the victims. Together they issued the following release, "In recent days we have seen the horror of a violent attack in a house of worship in Charleston. Tonight, in Kuwait City the seven of us attended events where we offered our condolences to the people of Kuwait following the horrific attack on the Al-Imam Al-Sadiq Mosque. The alliance between the United States and Kuwait is deeply important to both nations and we stand with our friends at this difficult time." Needless to say, this was a powerful moment for our two countries.

Although Kuwait came out strong and unified against this hateful act of terror, the tiny Gulf country cannot afford to rest against the threat of sectarianism. Unfortunately, there are those who live in Kuwait who harbor extremist beliefs and support acts of violence. They survive on the edges of Kuwaiti society. They hail from both sects of Islam. Authorities are aware of their presence but these extremists are difficult to find. Every once and awhile the government's vigilance pays off.

On August 13, 2015, not long after the ISIS bombing at the Shi'a mosque, Kuwaiti authorities uncovered a weapons cache smuggled through Iraq and hidden beneath three houses near the Iraqi border. A total of 19,000 kilograms of ammunition, 144 kilograms of explosives, 68 weapons, and 204 grenades were seized, according to the Kuwaiti Ministry of Interior sourced in an Al-Jazeera report. Three Kuwaiti citizens were arrested and confessed to joining a cell that allegedly was linked to Iran-backed Shi'a Hezbollah. The investigation has since lead to further arrests with more Kuwaiti citizens exposing their ties to Iran and Hezbollah.[clxiv] Truly, this tiny country is caught between extremists on both sides of the Shi'a - Sunni divide.

# CHAPTER SEVENTEEN

## *Education Can Help Bridge the Divide*

In an inspiring editorial written following the June 2015 bombing of the Shi'a mosque in downtown Kuwait, Brown University-educated and renowned Kuwaiti author Mai Al-Nakib questioned the country's current education system and its ability to prevent future violence over religious differences. Both she and her parents were educated in a more "secular" education system in Kuwait, Al-Nakib wrote, prior to what she referred to as the establishment of a "Sunni Islamist" curriculum now being taught in government schools. She faulted Kuwaiti schools for "educating children to care about trivial religious differences that did not previously matter much to the majority of Kuwaitis."[clxv]

"School should be the place where children are exposed to the world," she wrote, "where they learn how to think critically and independently; where they become curious and engaged; where they explore diversity and difference; and where the sciences, arts, and humanities are not short changed. Islam among other religions can be taught in religion class. But Islamism cannot be permitted to infiltrate every single subject or to determine what can be thought and said or to limit the kinds of books made available in school libraries. Islamists --

Salafist, Wahhabist, Muslim Brotherhood -- cannot be the sole ideology at work on young Kuwaiti minds."[clxvi]

If Mai Al-Nakib is right, neglecting to teach children to respect other cultures and religions, or worse, fomenting extremist views within one's own religion, has consequences, including for expats like us who live in the country. I heard several American community parents, who had children enrolled in private schools teaching the American curriculum, complain their children were taunted for not following the same religion or not looking like everyone else. Although these schools were private and welcomed the expatriate community, they were still under the jurisdiction of the Ministry of Education. Was this behavior the result of schools placing so much emphasis on Sunni Islamist and nationalist conditioning that children, who were neither Sunni nor Kuwaiti, were more vulnerable and more susceptible to bullying?

I never heard bullying was prevalent but when an instance occurred, it was often about kids not accepting someone for being different. Sometimes it was about an American girl teased for having blond hair; other times, it was about an American boy teased for being Christian. Frankly, I had never before heard students in an international school comment about their religious differences in other countries I had lived. Yes, there was bullying but I do not recall ever hearing comments regarding a child's religion. My experience has been that international schools that U.S. embassy and other foreign diplomat kids attend embrace and celebrate their diverse student bodies. Somehow it seemed that even the international schools in Kuwait were entangled with the Ministry of Education's desire to promote loyalty to the nation and their religion above teaching the message of tolerance and embracing the essential beauty of diversity.

Many of the people involved in the effort to promote Islamism in the Ministry of Education have come from Sunni Islamist backgrounds from abroad. A large number came from Egypt to pursue their religious, political, and social beliefs acquired from the Muslim Brotherhood, an Islamist political organization banned in their own country. They started coming to Kuwait in the seventies and eighties as job opportunities in the Gulf multiplied with the increase in oil wealth. As teachers, they were welcomed by the newly minted Kuwaiti citizens moving into Kuwait City from their desert camps along the Saudi border. These Bedouin Kuwaitis favored the conservative social and religious views of many of the expat teachers. The Bedouin Kuwaitis had the clout to hire these teachers because they had managed to plant themselves in the "lifestyle" government ministries, such as the Ministry of Education, and slowly and methodically, spawned an Islamist movement within the school system.

It seems to have happened under the noses of the liberal Kuwaiti merchant class without their noticing until it was too late. The Islamists have been enormously successful, writing textbooks and hiring conservative teachers from abroad, to make an indelible mark on the country's current education system.[clxvii] As a result, schools have adopted a more religious and nationalistic approach.[clxviii] Teaching respect for the physical, cultural and spiritual differences of people around the world became less important. Instead, students learned to recognize differences among their peers, whether they were Kuwaiti or non-Kuwaiti, Muslim or non-Muslim, and sadly, and more dangerously, Shi'a or Sunni.[clxix] Seeking to control diversity of thinking and beliefs within the student body comes at the expense of understanding and accepting of others; this I believe has helped enable extremist views.

Aside from the social implications of an Islamist-influenced education system on children, there are academic limitations in teaching within its framework. I saw this first hand. On the first day of our son's Philosophy class, for example, the American teacher handed out his textbook. But then she dropped the bombshell, telling the students that there were three chapters stapled shut in each book and warned her class not to open them under any circumstances. The teacher implored her students to comply with her request, explaining she would lose her job if they did not. We ordered a copy of the book from the Internet to see what the chapters were about. The chapters addressed *God, the Cosmos,* and *Death*; topics that could not be discussed outside of student's Islamic religion course, a course that non-Muslims were not permitted to take.

It was unlikely the Muslim students in their Islamic religion classes would discuss these three chapters either. Philosophers who might present competing ideas that could challenge the teachings of Islam and question faith wrote them. This is something that Islamists do not tolerate. The idea that students in Kuwait, including my own son, were not allowed to have their beliefs challenged bothered me. I was not pleased that my son was being denied the opportunity to learn about what the world's great philosophers thought about matters of the spirit and God. I wanted him to be challenged so that he could sharpen his own views and be better prepared for the world of competing ideas he would confront in college.

An American woman married to a Kuwaiti, who sent her five children through Kuwaiti public schools, told me once that what is most needed, in her opinion, is for the education system to teach about other religions and encourage religious tolerance. She was disappointed to learn that her children's public schools only focused on Islam without including studies about the world's other great monotheistic, Abrahamic religions. This would expand children's horizons and bring greater intercultural and interreligious awareness to the citizenry. The fact that her own children have learned to respect their father's religion of Islam as well as her own Christianity have made her children, according to my friend, more accepting and understanding. She believes this is a great gift that helps them daily.

Although she is very grateful for her life in Kuwait where she has raised her large and beautiful family, there have been occasions when she has had to be vigilant about where to send her children to learn. This is true everywhere. There are always adults ready to reach into children's minds to mold them according to their own points of view. When my friend sent her daughters to summer camp with a popular Kuwaiti Muslim youth organization for girls, she intended for them to learn arts and crafts as well as how to read the Qur'an. Instead, in the car on the way home, her daughters spoke of concern for family members in the States, fearing they would burn in hell because they were not Muslims. This is what their camp instructors had told them. The girls also told their mother that some of the counselors spoke negatively about the United States in a way that made them feel uncomfortable and unwelcome since their mother was American. Many of the camp instructors were Palestinians and Egyptians who were displeased with U.S. policies at the time. It was the 1990's and although the United States had led the way in liberating Kuwait, there were many in the Arab world who did not support U.S. intervention in the region. My friend decided to pull her daughters from the camp. She did not want them to be raised disrespecting other religions or the country she was born, the United States.

The teaching of evolution was also not permitted in Kuwaiti schools, though there were exceptions when it came to AP Biology class in private schools. This policy was based on the religious premise that God created man and that teaching science challenging this belief would be un-Islamic. Advocates of this policy, however, did not seem to realize that failing to teach evolution puts students at a disadvantage if they wish to study higher level science or pursue a scientific career in the future. This Islamist influence, however, in the education system does not permeate through the rest of Kuwaiti society. For example, Kuwait's premier scientific institutes, such as the Dasman Diabetes Institute, are heavily involved in scientific research dependent on the science of evolution. So, while Islamists have managed to influence the education system in the country, they do not prevail over Kuwaiti society. There are safeguards preventing this from happening, including the ruling family itself, which has deep authority and support in the country. But still, even as the ruling family continues to invest in progressive infrastructure to push their country forward, having such a conservative and Islamist-influenced education system will make it more difficult for the leadership to modernize the country. Now more than ever, Kuwait must have schools educating children with open and creative minds to power an economy that is not just dependent on oil.

Kuwaitis want to have it both ways. A Kuwaiti businesswoman one day said she wanted her children educated so that they could work anywhere in the world. Composed and confident in her pristine white headscarf, she was a modern mom who advocated strong parental involvement in raising and educating kids. She talked about how she read books on rearing successful children from the moment her own were born. She mentioned prominent pediatrician and author Dr. Benjamin Spock, but conceded that some of the theories he wrote in the 1940's and 50's were no longer valid. Then she said something really interesting. Recently she had read a book about how the Prophet Muhammad believed children should be raised and radiantly noted that everything he said made perfect sense. The simplicity of his ideas on childrearing, she said, are as relevant today as they were hundreds of years ago. I had images of 7th century Arabia in my head, but decided not to ask how the experiences of that time and place could apply in today's world. This was, after all, a matter of faith.

Kuwaitis have a split personality when it comes to what they want for their children and their education. People are divided about whether children should be educated in a way that preserves Kuwait's national identity, culture, and religion, or that cultivates knowledge and creativity to equip them to succeed in a global economy.[clxx] For the moment, it appears the forces that want to preserve Kuwait's traditions have the upper hand. The country's curriculum has become focused on Arabic language, Islam, and the Arab world, while the study of math, science, history, and culture of other regions of the world must accommodate these central needs.

Kuwaiti children, like children all over the world, are reminded of the importance of being loyal to their country from the moment they arrive at school. Both public and private school children line up each morning to raise the flag to the sound of the Kuwaiti national anthem, but in public schools, children also hear selected texts from the Qur'an.[clxxi] Proponents of this practice believe their Islamic faith is the surest way to guarantee Kuwait's future prosperity and security. These Kuwaitis see their religion as a moral and just way to live and believe the best place for children to learn to be good Muslims is in the schools. Therefore, Islam should be taught throughout their children's education and that such an education will nurture an orderly and values-oriented society. In Kuwait, religion is a required course for all Muslim children, no matter in which school they are enrolled; instruction about the existence of other religious beliefs, as my friend noted, is not provided.

Kuwait's senior leadership, however, is well aware of the negative effects levied on its youth from teachers who harbor extreme and exclusive beliefs. Unfortunately, extremism has been a part of the landscape in the Middle East and in the Gulf for the past few decades. With so much extremism in the region, fed by failures in political systems to address corrupt economies and poverty, the entire world is now feeling the results. The 21st century has witnessed a dangerous increase in terror at the hands of religious extremists using Islam to try to legitimize their criminal and inhuman actions. They have managed to spread their views everywhere, most dangerously among youth.

I can think of no more dramatic example than ISIS's occupation of Mosul that began in 2014, a culturally diverse city in northern Iraq. Now, in the aftermath of Mosul's liberation, a top focus for Iraq is addressing the psychological state of the thousands of children who were exposed to the violence of ISIS ideology. In some instances, young boys, many of them from the Yezidi community, were forced into ISIS schools to learn their barbarous techniques of occupation, including even how to behead. These children in particular need the care of experts to help them rehabilitate back into society.[clxxii] Whether it is through formalized education or the fostering of ideas at home, children and youth are shaped today for the future they will live. It is important to consider how education can help advance acceptance of social and religious diversity so that countries can stand firm against threats from those who wish to sow seeds of intolerance, either from outside or from within.

# CHAPTER EIGHTEEN

## *Be Careful What You Wish For*

In addition to addressing curriculum issues related to religious tolerance, Kuwait has also been taking a closer look at how it can prepare its youth to achieve greater success in studying in higher education institutions abroad. Many Kuwaiti students have been struggling and not performing at the necessary level to succeed at the foreign institutions where they were studying. It was not surprising to learn this since Kuwaiti public schools in general have been lagging behind due to a less rigorous and dated educational curriculum, particularly in the STEM subjects of science, technology, engineering and math.

Kuwaitis can generally afford to go to the United States and elsewhere to obtain good educations through the country's generous scholarship funds. However, the Kuwaiti government does not want to waste these scholarships. Thus, Kuwaiti education officials decided to raise the academic standards, including English language skills, required to receive these generous scholarships. The hope was that Kuwaiti students would have a better chance at successfully completing their degrees, especially those studying in more rigorous programs.

It is not easy to study in a foreign country in a different educational system. But if students are neither prepared academically nor equipped with the necessary English language skills, they are most likely headed for failure. The teaching of English overseas, especially in countries in the Middle East, is really important. Not only does it provide opportunities for Arab students to study in the United States, it enhances cultural understanding and communication between countries. I learned to appreciate this as the Director of the American Language Center (ALC) in Amman, Jordan, my job when we lived there from 2000 to 2004. In my view, teaching English is one of the most valuable and useful efforts our government can undertake overseas.

To attract more qualified students, the Ministry of Higher Education in Kuwait decided in 2015 to raise officially the grade point average (GPA) required to apply for their highly coveted government scholarships to study in the U.S. from B- to a solid B. This decision, however, resulted in fewer Kuwaiti students qualifying for the scholarships to study in the States. According to an official of the Ministry, during the 2014-2015 academic year, there were 2,400 Kuwaiti freshmen students studying in the States. In the 2015-2016 school year after the new standard was applied, there were only 1,600 freshmen going to study in the States on scholarship. The decrease in students was a direct result of the raised grade point requirement.

Although it may not necessarily be good for the bottom line of American universities and colleges, it is ultimately wise for U.S. academic institutions to accept only qualified students from abroad. A *New York Times* article on March 21, 2016, highlighted the academic challenges that can arise when there are a large number of students from the Gulf in public universities in rural America who may not necessarily be properly prepared to succeed in school.[clxxiii] According to the article, a large number of students from Kuwait and Saudi Arabia had enrolled in engineering programs at Idaho State University in Pocatello. Their professors soon realized that many did not have the proper academic skills, particularly in math, to pass their courses. Accusations of cheating began to circulate and the situation grew untenable.

Compounding matters in Pocatello, however, were also misunderstandings surrounding religion and cultural pastimes such as hookah smoking and car racing. Local relations became strained between the students enrolled in Idaho State and the local community. Racist actions on the part of a few locals and several burglaries of foreign student apartments and vehicles eventually led many Kuwaiti and Saudi students to look elsewhere to complete their education. This story certainly behooves college and university administrators to consider more carefully the overall qualifications of admitting foreign students who can afford paying the full price for their education.

During the annual conference of the National Union of Kuwaiti Students USA (NUKS USA), one of the Kuwaiti students shared his strategy to qualify for a coveted scholarship to study at a U.S. university. He said that although it was more difficult to obtain a B average in a private school, he chose to go because the curriculum would be taught in English. In public schools, where it probably would have been easier, he would have had to study in Arabic. For him personally, he felt that studying in Kuwaiti public schools would not have prepared him to study abroad. There are a large number of private schools in Kuwait that teach in English and incorporate western curriculums. Many Kuwaitis, who can afford the steep fees of these private schools, ranging from about 3,000 KD (almost $10,000) for kindergarten and up to 7,000 KD (over $23,000) for high school, attend in the hope of getting a college scholarship. This puts enormous pressure on private school educators.[clxxiv]

The Superintendent of the American School of Kuwait (ASK), which has the distinction of being accredited in the United States by the Middle States Association of Colleges and Schools, once told me that if she could change one thing in the Kuwaiti education system, it would be getting rid of the scholarship requiring a B average.[clxxv] She believes this policy encourages Kuwaiti students to shy away from taking more difficult honors and AP courses offered at ASK. Their primary concern was always their grade point average. Add parental pressure, and it was challenging for private school teachers from the United States, Britain, and Canada to grade their students. While the teachers wanted to instill the desire to learn in their students, they often found themselves up against students who only want to achieve a B average instead.

To avoid situations like what happened at Idaho State in Pocatello, the Ministry of Higher Education is careful to spread Kuwaiti students around the U.S. The ministry tries not to put more than 50 Kuwaiti students at a single university. The last thing it wants is for Kuwaitis to hang around each other all day and lose the opportunity to learn about Americans and their way of life. The ministry wants their students to immerse themselves in the college experience while in the States, but with some caveats. Kuwaiti students, male and female, do not generally live in dormitories like other freshmen on campus. Kuwaiti parents were not comfortable with the freshman dorm experience, especially for their daughters. Thus, most Kuwaiti students live off campus in apartments. Many parents bought condominiums not far away from campus and lived with their students while they attended college.

When it came to their daughters going to the United States to study at the young age of 18, many Kuwaiti parents told me they preferred for them to wait until they were more mature. They said they would, however, consider sending their daughters to graduate school in the States. I asked the Ministry of Higher Education official about scholarships given to Kuwaiti women. The official assured me that plenty of young Kuwaiti women were also participating in the scholarship program. I did see a number of bright and independent female graduates at the NUKS conference, but it did seem that the vast majority present were men.

Those Kuwaiti students who successfully graduated from U.S. universities were an impressive group of young people. It cannot be overstated how much an education in the United States can affect these students once they return to Kuwait. They brim with confidence and knowledge that they received the best education possible. At the NUKS USA conference, I couldn't help but notice how these Kuwaiti graduates spoke to each other. Their Arabic was constantly interrupted with American expressions. It was the first time I heard this hybrid language spoken in Kuwait. It was as if this group of graduates had forged their own tribe and its own way to communicate. I enjoyed hearing the graduates boast about which university they attended or in which state they studied. I could hear the subtle twang of a mid-western grad and see the preppy dress of an east coast one. Practically every state was represented. Many of these students bring back with them the desire to pursue careers that utilize their educations and critical thinking skills. They are the ones who were most prepared to be a part of the robust private sector that the government envisions. The challenge was that it was still tough to find careers outside the government and there were not many new positions within the government to be had either.

On a flight to Kuwait from Washington in September 2015, I had the opportunity to sit next to a thirty-something Kuwaiti gentleman. He worked as a manager in the Kuwaiti fire department, an important government job when you think of all the fires that happen in Kuwait City. (I say this because Kuwaiti Instagrammers post a lot of photos of fires around Kuwait City, especially in the summer.) He was returning from Los Angeles dressed in designer shorts, T-shirt and blue suede Topsiders. He had been assisting his nephew in settling into an English language program there to prepare him to study at a California university. The family wanted to give him every opportunity to succeed.

I was pleased to hear that, since it is not easy to come from abroad and just drop into our competitive American higher education system, never mind getting accustomed to the freedom of living in the States. Although I have talked about how the Kuwaiti government offers scholarships to Kuwaitis who do well in school, I have not mentioned their monthly stipends and how generous they are. Having so much money each month can be a challenge for any young person living on their own for the first time. An American friend told me that the president of the University of Virginia counseled incoming freshmen parents of the class of 2019 that students did not require more than $100 a month to live comfortably at college, noting that student living expenses had already been paid for since they were living in dormitories and eating campus food. Unlike American freshmen, however, Kuwaiti students rent apartments and have a significant amount of cash to support themselves. I understand they have a monthly allowance for miscellaneous expenses in addition to the money they receive to pay their tuition and rent. These miscellaneous funds can range from $3,000 to $5,000 per month.[clxxvi] I shudder to think how the generous Kuwaiti allowances are spent. One popular way to spend the money is leasing or buying very expensive cars. Another way is to travel. Many of these students are able to see a good deal of the United States with their monthly cash infusions.

The fashionable Kuwaiti fireman then talked about what Kuwaiti students might expect to find when they returned to their country armed with their U.S. degrees. He was not very upbeat. Recent college graduates from the States as well as from private colleges in Kuwait were not having an easy time finding a job. Typically, when Kuwaitis graduate college, they are guaranteed a job but must first submit their names to the government to be placed on a national registry. In the past, these graduates would be quickly offered jobs somewhere in the public sector. Today, it is taking a very long time for the government to find jobs for newly minted graduates. The whole system is under great pressure with some 9,000 names on the list.[clxxvii] He had heard of several cases where the government has begun sending anxious graduates who have been on the registry for more than a year to obscure office spaces to work. When these young grads show up, they find they are only in these offices to collect a salary without having to do a thing. There is no real work to be done because these offices are facades. Eventually the new "employees" realize they are not contributing anything and that their paycheck is for doing almost nothing.

Kuwait is blessed with amazing wealth but it does not necessarily guarantee happiness, at least not without a good deal of anxiety and disappointment. While it was gratifying to meet so many impressive college graduates in Kuwait, there were plenty of other Kuwaitis who were not as blessed with the virtue of hard work. Somehow this virtue had eluded them as children. While parents may have not always been able to do the best job teaching them the importance of hard work at home, their children were often not learning this important virtue in school either.

Whether parents came from conservative religious families or liberal merchant families, they all worried about the impact of wealth on their children's character and wellbeing. One evening during dinner at our residence, an American investment banker involved in wealth management for extremely rich families exclaimed, "How fortunate to be Kuwaiti! If everyone could have their problems." Later, she confided that her Kuwaiti clients were very apprehensive about giving their children so much money. They worried how wealth would affect their children's lives, whether it would expose them to incessant family squabbles instead of love and joy. They wondered what kind of people their children would become when they realized they would not have to work for their living.

Of course, there are plenty of Kuwaiti youth who want to work hard to acquire knowledge and be productive members of society regardless of their wealth. This is borne out in the country's impressive literacy rates, its equal access to education for both girls and boys, and the plethora of academic options throughout the country in both public and private schools. Kuwait is a beacon in the region in terms of educating women. A full 70 percent of the student body at Kuwait University is female. Nonetheless, I kept hearing from parents and teachers concerns about the overall commitment of Kuwaiti students to learn. The comments of a longtime teacher in the Kuwaiti school system summed up the problem best. In his editorial in Kuwait's *Friday Times* in June 2016, Samer Yousef Abualrub, said his students simply "lacked motivation." A majority of students, he said, would not bother to come to class at all if their parents did not make them.[clxxviii] For many Kuwaiti children, school was merely a place to be bored, a place to flaunt their Rolex watches and cell phones, and remind their teachers they would one day have good jobs in the government whether they studied or not.[clxxix]

Instead of learning the material in the classroom, students often relied on paid tutors to provide private instruction at home.[clxxx] Teachers were well aware of the problem of private tutoring. They could see the difference in the neat homework handed in and the work produced by students in class.[clxxxi] I heard several American teachers talk about their experiences in teaching Kuwaiti students. They described Kuwaiti students regularly entering class unprepared, without pencils and paper. They had no intention of participating because they knew their tutors would help them later. Some students were content just to receive the passing grade of D so they could move to the next grade.

Parents sometimes did not do their part to make sure their younger children were ready to participate in class either. When an elementary teacher asked her students to bring cooking items to class for a special cooking lesson, a couple of Kuwaiti students did not bother because their moms told them they would never cook in their lives anyway.[clxxxii] Nonetheless, teachers felt parents held them responsible for their children's work rather than the children themselves. When their kids failed, parents blamed their teachers. Providing final grades was like bargain hunting in a grand bazaar with parents haggling over final numeric scores. One teacher said he was offered a car once if he would agree to change a student's grade. School administrators have had to step in on numerous occasions and take responsibility for issuing report card results due to the pressures of parents. If parents were particularly connected to powerful entities, known in Arabic as having *wasta*, they could be particularly overbearing and manage to get their way.

In younger grades, nannies and drivers coddled the children. A teacher once overheard in dismay a schoolboy calling his driver on the cell phone to have his tea ready for the ride home.[clxxxiii] At pick up time, Asian nannies lined up at the gates to receive the children. Kuwaiti parents were often nowhere in sight, too busy to collect the children themselves, either working or preparing for the family's midday meal. Lunch around 2:30 p.m. is sacrosanct in Kuwait and it always seemed that virtually every family member was on the road returning home. There were intrepid Kuwaiti parents who bravely drove to school to retrieve their children, but given the mass traffic disorder that prevailed whenever schools let out, picking up children would not necessarily be something any parent would necessarily want to do.

Without actually going through the rigor of learning in secondary school, many of these privileged Kuwaiti students enter college without the necessary skills to succeed. Their writing is weak, and they lack the ability to express themselves to support their arguments and ideas.[clxxxiv] Nor do they have the proper research and analytical skills. According to several parents, this is true in the English language as well as in Arabic. Perhaps this is because both languages are used in the education system with little coordination. Public schools are required to teach in Arabic. Private schools teach in English or other foreign languages. In the higher education system in Kuwait, both Arabic and English are used depending on the subject. Add this muddle to uninspiring textbooks and a lack of critical thinking, and the whole system could use a new approach.

Plagiarism has also become relatively commonplace. Currently, according to a Kuwait University professor, plagiarism is not a punishable offense in public schools including at the university level. Students freely copy and paste original work found on the Internet because they know their teachers and administrators will not challenge them, especially for work submitted in English. They are not challenged because teachers are often not proficient enough in the English language themselves. In the view of this Kuwaiti professor, no matter how Kuwait University strives to modernize, it will not be a true center for research and scholarship without preventing plagiarism. To their credit, private secondary schools in Kuwait forbid plagiarism and require teachers to check students' work through websites like *Turnitin.com*. This is why Kuwaitis who graduate from private schools generally have better writing skills in the English language and are better prepared to attend universities abroad. Many parents choose to send their children to private schools for this reason, even though they incur huge expenses from the high tuition.

It should not be surprising then that the quality of education in Kuwait has retreated in international education rankings. According to the Kuwait Times, Kuwait ranked 106th in a list of 148 countries in 2013-14, losing 18 positions compared to 2010-2011. The low rankings were attributed to teaching methods focused on dictation and memorization and a general lack of fostering creativity and critical thinking.[clxxxv] Parents, teachers, and school administrators need to work together to improve this ranking. Parents should consider spending more time reading to their children, helping them with homework, and instilling in them the necessary discipline and respect to succeed in school. Schools, on the other hand, need to make the school day more interesting, inspiring, and innovative.[clxxxvi]

I met many Kuwaitis both inside and outside the government who regarded their education system as critical for preparing their children for happy and productive lives. Kuwait's Minister of Education and Minister of Higher Education, Dr. Bader Hamad Al-Essa, appointed in 2015, has been working hard to develop new standards of education, including advancing a more inclusive civics curriculum and hiring qualified teachers to teach it.[clxxxvii] He wanted children to become responsible citizens who could think critically and collaborate, and solve problems together in a democratic society. He also wanted their teachers to emulate behaviors that promoted this. Dr. Al-Essa, who chose to appear in public in a western business suit rather than the traditional white *dishdasha*, has a Ph.D. in Sociology from a university in the States. I met him once and it was clear from our brief encounter that he understood how a national education system affects society and its future generations.

At a Gulf Cooperation Council (GCC) meeting of Education Ministers in Riyadh in April 2016, he presented a Kuwaiti plan to promote good citizenship in schools by supplanting school curricula that enabled sectarianism and extremism for one that embraced pluralism and tolerance.[clxxxviii] The other Gulf countries agreed to adapt the plan as well. It was clear from the press article these educational leaders were ready to take a stand against extremists, alarmed their dangerous views had managed to infiltrate their education systems through teachers who were proponents. It appeared they were ready to take the reins on education and stand up against extremism.

This does not mean that he and the other Gulf education ministers were seeking to separate Islam from their education systems. On the contrary, Muslims do not see their religion as radical at all. They see the problem as a human problem where the wrong people have tried to use Islam to gain influence and power, and have seriously distorted the religion. They want to take back their religion, and they want their education system to reflect Islam's essential ethical character in their children's education. In fact, of the eight competences to be mastered by Kuwaiti students in the 12th grade, the Islamic Religious and Ethical Competence is number one.[clxxxix] What is different in the new curriculum is that teaching this competency now involves emphasizing the need to show respect and appreciation for other religions and other beliefs. Educators are required now to encourage their students to understand and be open to other cultures.[cxc] The objective is to heal sectarian and religious divides within the country, including the divide between the Sunni and Shi'a. Only time will tell if this new policy will succeed. Formal emphasis on Islam in schools, at the exclusion of other religions and beliefs, is still likely to present challenges for children to be truly open and accepting of others. Thus, it remains important for people to stay involved in what their children are learning -- as it is everywhere in the world -- especially when they are not a member of the community that has ultimate authority over the system.

# CHAPTER NINETEEN

## *Taking the Reins*

An American mom married to a Kuwaiti wanted to do just that when she took the trouble to deliver three different school textbooks to the American embassy. She had two children enrolled in the Kuwaiti school system and was flabbergasted several years ago when they had showed her their social studies books and what the books taught about Saddam Hussein's invasion of Kuwait. Although her children had long since graduated, she decided to paper clip and highlight the paragraphs addressing the 1990 invasion and bring the books to the U.S. embassy not long before we arrived in August 2014. She wanted the embassy to know how little was being taught, at least in these particular textbooks, about how Americans fought and sacrificed to prevent Kuwait from becoming the 19th province of Iraq.

Doug was made aware of the textbooks the first day he walked into his office. His deputy, Joey Hood, had stacked the three Arabic language textbooks on the center of his desk so he could not miss them. The books had only recently made their way up to the executive office after having gone through several hands. At the front gate, security officers screened them for suspicious content. Then, various embassy officers perused them to determine whether they warranted senior attention. In this age of high security, it is not easy to deliver something to the embassy without a great deal of scrutiny. But had this concerned mom not brought the books, our diplomats may never have known to focus on youth to mark the occasion of the 25th Anniversary of the liberation of Kuwait. The jubilee anniversary was due to take place on February 26, 2016, and Doug wanted to make the commemoration a centerpiece of his tenure.

I was surprised to learn that the schoolbooks did not highlight the bravery of the Kuwaiti people during the invasion, much less the role of U.S. forces. Hundreds of martyrs had died during the invasion. As horrible as it was, the invasion demonstrated incredible fortitude and courage of all those who remained in Kuwait at the time. I simply could not fathom that Kuwaiti educators would allow those who endured the menacing threats of Saddam's soldiers, who pillaged their homes and neighborhoods, be forgotten. Saddam's soldiers subjected the Kuwaitis and expats left behind to frightening random searches in which children sometimes watched loved ones dragged from their beds as hostages, or worse, brutally killed in front of them.[cxci] It was a seriously dangerous time, requiring the utmost cunning just to find food and water to stay alive. How could their heroism be let go?

I had the opportunity to take a quick look at the textbooks and sure enough, I found little to honor the memory.[cxcii] The authors of these textbooks for some reason decided to gloss over the entire experience. There was quick reference to the fact that the invasion happened, but the books oddly credited only the neighboring Arab and Islamic countries in the country's liberation. The United States was not even mentioned. This was what concerned the American mom with the Kuwaiti children, and my husband, the most.

Perhaps the authors found the experience of the invasion too humiliating. Perhaps, they felt it was best not to remind students that forces outside the Muslim world, "infidels," had come to their country's rescue to turn back the violent aggression of a neighboring Arab "brother." Islamists, who had gained power in the post-1990 era, certainly would not champion such a narrative. These post-1990 schoolbooks also may have simply reflected Kuwait's overwhelming desire to survive and rebuild itself. It probably was easier to write as little as possible about the war so as not to provoke any of its powerful neighbors, not just Iraq, but also Saudi Arabia and Iran. Whatever the case, I applauded the American mom for coming forward. It would be wrong for Kuwaiti children not to learn about their history and about some of the heroes who emerged from that most difficult time in Kuwait history -- heroes like Engineer Sara Akbar.

I first became aware of her when I saw the documentary film *Fires of Kuwait* in the IMAX Theater at Kuwait's Scientific Center where the film is shown regularly. As a young engineer employed by KOC, she was on the ground assisting the Kuwaiti well fire team, one of many firefighting teams who also came from around the world to put out the raging fires in 1991. Saddam's defeated soldiers had set the oil wells on fire as they departed. Her detailed knowledge of the oil wells was instrumental in helping the firefighters snuff out the fires in just nine months. She won international acclaim for her bravery and determination and was made famous with her participation in the 1992 documentary that was nominated for an Academy Award for Best Documentary Feature.

She came to speak at one of our international women's group events. At the lectern, Sara told us about her childhood during which she learned a lot about oil because her dad worked at the Burgan oil field. She was the only daughter in a family of four siblings and learned how to work with men since she hung around her brothers and their friends so much. This helped her a great deal in working later as an engineer at KOC after receiving her engineering degree from Kuwait University. She had already worked at KOC for 10 years by the time Saddam Hussein's troops rolled into Kuwait on August 2, 1990.

I was thrilled to sit next to her at the lunch that followed. She humbly told me that had she not gone through the war, there would have been a good chance she would never have come to prominence. Following the invasion, she stayed at the state-owned KOC for another 10 years but then decided to take a risk. With her celebrity and experience, she decided to establish her own private oil company with two other business partners. The name of her company is the Kuwait Energy Company. As Kuwait only permits the state run KOC to work in the oil sector in Kuwaiti territory, her company focuses on operations outside the country in challenging locations including Egypt, Yemen, Pakistan, Oman, and Iraq. Ironically, among her company's most significant achievements, is that it struck oil in southern Iraq in 2014 from a concession and exploration license obtained from the Iraqi Ministry of Oil in 2012.[cxciii]

At a dinner, we hosted at our home in January 2016, Sara told us the interesting story about her company's discovery of oil at that concession outside of Basrah which is also the largest discovery of oil in Iraq in 30 years. When Kuwait Energy received the exploration license and concession, it hired the Iraqi Drilling Company to set up the rig to do the drilling. On the first try, Sara and her company struck oil. The irony was that the rig used was the same rig that Sara used to work on when she worked in the Kuwaiti oil fields at KOC. She fondly called it *Rig No. 10* and she recognized every part. She even remembered painting it. When she inquired about the rig to the Iraqi Drilling Company, the Iraqi management admitted that Iraqi soldiers had taken the rig from Kuwait during the 1990 invasion. The Iraqi company sheepishly explained that the financial concessions paid by their government to the Kuwaitis at the end of the war covered the cost of the rig, making it their own.

Sara is an anomaly in her generation with her strong belief in the power of the private sector. She is truly a unique story. After 35 years of working in the energy sector, she also has goals beyond just finding and extracting oil. She wants to change lives, empower women, and keep the environment clean. She is especially interested in the welfare of Iraq's southern city of Basrah. Many Kuwaitis share historic familial ties with the people from this city located not more than a two-hour drive away from Kuwait City. Recently, she has been particularly concerned about the level of public services being provided to the citizens of Basrah, specifically about trash collection. She proposed starting up a private trash collection service in Basrah using assets from her company set aside for reinvestment in Iraq. She hoped the service would provide jobs for the local people as well as help clean up the city. She later reported that she had not been able to get her initiative off the ground. She could not guarantee that her company's assets would not be used to line the pockets of corrupt individuals who would somehow get access to the money and divert it from its intended use to clean up the garbage.[cxciv] Nonetheless, Sara is an important role model in business as well as in her compassion and willingness to forgive.

Clearly, Kuwaiti students needed to reflect on their history, not only to learn about heroes like Sara Akbar and the strength of Kuwaiti character, but also about the special friendship and shared history Kuwait has with the United States. Their studies should recognize the significant role the United States had in liberating their nation. For our Embassy, 18 months remained before the 25th Anniversary would be officially marked, and much work needed to be done to make sure this happened. U.S. diplomats do not normally involve themselves in local schools, but it is their job to maintain good relations between the United States and the country to which they are assigned. Kuwait has become a key partner in maintaining stability in the Gulf, and today, is host of the fourth largest U.S. overseas military presence in the world, behind Germany, Japan, and South Korea.[cxcv] To guarantee this hugely important relationship into the future, my husband decided the U.S. embassy needed to focus on preserving the history of the United States coming to Kuwait's aid 25 years ago by celebrating the occasion directly in the country's schools.

Fortunately, the Political-Military affairs officer assigned to the Embassy at the time was a former high school teacher in Texas before she decided to become a Foreign Service Officer. There have not been many Political-Military Officers with her background that I have known. Typically, they have been former lawyers, military officers, or have advanced degrees in foreign languages and regional studies. As a former teacher, she knew what needed to be done to get students actively learning more about their history. She decided to organize an education campaign to be held in schools across Kuwait, including speeches, performances, and various art competitions commemorating the crisis of 1990-1991. She encouraged students to seek out family, friends, and neighbors who lived through Saddam's occupation and the liberation, and interview them on video. Their videos would then be entered into a competition to be viewed by judges and their classmates to determine the best ones. By preserving the memory of the experiences of people who survived the war on video, students would permanently document their history so that future generations would never forget their country's heroes.[cxcvi] It was now or never because those who experienced the war firsthand as adults would not be around much longer. Time was passing. Our officer also envisioned bringing U.S. service members and her civilian colleagues from the U.S. embassy to participate in school-wide assemblies. First, she needed the approval and support of the Kuwaiti government.

Approval and support came swiftly. My husband could not have been more pleased. The Kuwaiti government advised him personally that they thought the idea to commemorate the 25th Anniversary of Kuwait's liberation in the schools was excellent. From their standpoint, it was essential to do this. To prove his support, Minister of Information Salman Sabah Al-Salem Al-Homoud Al-Sabah tasked his ministry to fund and work with an American company to produce a documentary film detailing the story of the liberation. He made available

500,000 copies for U.S. veterans' organizations so that it could be seen across the United States.[cxcvii] He understood how important it was for Kuwaitis to show their deep appreciation for all the American soldiers' efforts to keep them free. The Ministry also distributed copies of the film and unused footage to Kuwaiti media outlets, so that Kuwaitis themselves could relive events and not forget the American and foreign forces who came to their assistance. Meanwhile, the Minister of Education, Dr. Al-Essa, asked several schools across Kuwait City to hold special events commemorating the 25th Anniversary and welcomed the participation of the U.S. embassy and their military colleagues.

After months of preparation, the first event took place on October 20, 2015. Members of the U.S. Embassy, the U.S. Central Command, and the Kuwaiti Ministry of Education assembled at the Fatima Bint Al-Waleed Girls High School. During the school assembly, the lively 82nd Airborne Division Band played popular American tunes while some of the high school musicians joined in. At other events, American female soldiers taught physical training to enthusiastic female students. American troops in the Medical Corps were invited to teach First Aid to children who welcomed the opportunity to learn life-saving skills. The U.S. military soldiers who participated were also delighted, especially those who had fought in places like Iraq and Afghanistan. They were touched to see the children's warmth and gratitude. One soldier commented how he felt so much better about having fought in these countries, now that he could see kids living in peace and going to school.[cxcviii]

The U.S. ambassador and the senior most American military officer assigned to the embassy, General Scott Williams, made sure to attend the numerous school events as much as their schedules permitted. The Kuwaitis also sent senior government officials to show their support at the school gatherings. I was also asked to participate. On November 22, 2015, I went to the Subai'a Bint Al-Hareth Al-Mutawaseta Banat School, a middle school for girls. I was thrilled to attend and delivered a speech in Arabic specially prepared by the embassy for the event. I talked about the sacrifices their relatives had made to defend their country and how my own dad had helped free Kuwait as a U.S. Army Medical Corps doctor who served in Operation Desert Storm. My parents later visited us in Kuwait for the 25th Anniversary of Kuwait's liberation in February 2016. While at the Kuwait House for National Works, a private museum commemorating the Kuwaiti martyrs who died in the war, my dad presented the uniform he had worn as commander of the 46th U.S. Army combat support hospital during the Gulf War. In return, one of the Kuwaitis at the museum took his shirt with the museum's emblem off his back and gave it to my dad as an expression of his sincere thanks.

After my speech at the girls' school, we watched the students deliver a live performance to mark the occasion. On a dark stage pierced with swirling lights accompanied by ominous music, the girls choreographed and danced the story of the brutal invasion, the taking of hostages, and the killing of loved ones. The performance ended with thanks and praise for the U.S. and multinational forces that fought to oust Saddam's soldiers, demonstrated in a jubilant parade of flags. Students carried written signs with the words love, cooperation, friendship, safety, and loyalty across the stage. The senior Kuwaiti Foreign Ministry official who attended the event, Ambassador Reem Al-Khaled, one of a handful of female ambassadors, was visibly moved. Tears had welled in her eyes, as she was old enough to remember the invasion personally.

We then went outside into the school courtyard. The senior female American General assigned in Kuwait and I prepared to receive small white doves to send into the air as a sign of peace. As the Kuwaiti handlers individually placed the doves in our hands, concerns of Avian Flu floated through my mind. But as we released the doves, it was amazing to see them fly high into the sky. I would not have wanted to miss this experience for the world. The girls then gathered around us for pictures and selfies. It was a beautiful event. They seemed so young and gentle to me, at the tender age of puberty when most began to wear their white headscarves. One girl gently held my hand and I will always remember her lovely smile.

Hopefully, these girls will do something similar every year to commemorate the horrible war and the brave people who lived through it, and know they have friends around the world who came to their rescue, including a big nation like the United States. I was grateful for the opportunity to have been welcomed into a Kuwaiti school to tell our story. The experience truly reflected Kuwait's open spirit, but it also proved that a U.S. Ambassador and his team of American diplomats have important roles to play in the nations to which they are assigned. Their efforts to safeguard U.S. interests overseas are critical, whether they concern bilateral ties, business and trade issues, political and military alliances, or the environment. Diplomatic engagement in other countries is likely to become more important in the 21st century as competition for influence intensifies; hopefully, Americans will continue to support their diplomats overseas, even though the appeal of isolationism may grow in the face of an ever more complicated world.

When it came time for me to leave Kuwait in August 2016, I was able to do so with a warm regard for its people and country. I am confident the Kuwaitis I met will help their country navigate the world in a thoughtful and peaceful way in which they will preserve their cherished culture while also enabling a dignified livelihood for all those who also call their country home. Kuwait is a potential role model for the region. It was a privilege and honor to serve there as the wife of the U.S. ambassador.

# EPILOGUE

I am now sitting inside the protective walls of the U.S. embassy compound in Baghdad, on the second floor of our home, overlooking the Tigris River that flows gently through the city, separating me from Iraq. I can just barely see the green palm trees and yellow marsh grasses lining the other side of the river where low-rise housing recedes into the haze of the rest of the city. Midway through our tour in Kuwait, Doug was asked to be the next U.S. Ambassador to Iraq and so we decided to forego our final year in Kuwait.

By the time Doug arrived in Baghdad in September 2016, the Iraqi military, with the help of U.S. and other military forces, was preparing to oust ISIS from Mosul, one of Iraq's largest cities occupied by ISIS since 2014. Doug became quickly engulfed in making sure all the players in the Iraqi government were on board with the battle plan, from the Prime Minister in Baghdad to the leaders in Iraqi Kurdistan Region. Equally important, he wanted humanitarian services ready and available for the hundreds of thousands of residents in Mosul who would no doubt run for their lives once the battle started in October.

I finally arrived in November. In the year that I have been here, I have already noticed many of the same challenges in Iraq that I saw in Kuwait. There are urban Iraqis and rural Iraqis, liberals and conservatives, women who cover and women who don't, and men who support women and men who hold them back, or worse, who beat them. The big difference in Iraq is that its problems are far greater because the country is so much larger, and the people are so much more divided along religious, ethnic, linguistic, and political lines that have hardened over centuries. The level of distrust in Iraq is extremely high, and fear about the future is palpable.

But in the same way that I met people in Kuwait who gave me hope, I have been meeting Iraqis working to improve their country. Many of them tell me they are working for a better Iraq for their children, especially now that ISIS has been defeated and forced from their country. They are so much more willing to work together now that they faced a common enemy. And because so many women suffered so severely at the hands of this common enemy, women are also emerging more empowered than ever before. This too is reason to believe that Iraq could one day be a prosperous nation again.

It would be a shame for the United States to leave Iraq now. Our continued support of Iraq is at a critical moment. With so much blood and treasure the United States has already sunk into Iraq, the United States should not cede its gains to other regional or international powers. We should continue to engage and work with Iraq and hopefully, our tenacity in this oil-rich and strategic country will lead to benefits for both nations. But as one who has an interest in the Iraqi people, I would love to see them recover from decades of war and authoritarian rule, and have Iraq become a country where future generations thrive and where the United States is perceived as a friend.

December 2017

# ABOUT THE AUTHOR

Catherine Raia Silliman grew up in Harvard, Massachusetts, but her earlier experience in Vicenza, Italy, where her father served in the U.S. army, opened her eyes to the possibilities of a world beyond her New England town. While in high school, she journeyed to Turkey as an American Field Service exchange student. That experience – pitting cherries and rolling grape leaves with Turkish women, feeling the tension between communists and nationalists, and hearing the calls to prayer from the minaret of the local mosque – enticed her to learn more. She earned a degree in International Relations from Tufts University, including a year abroad at the American University in Cairo. After a stint as a reporter for a Saudi Arabian newspaper in Washington, D.C., she got a degree in Middle Eastern Studies from the University of Chicago before launching into three decades of living and working in the Middle East and South Asia.

# END NOTES

[i] Lawrence, Bruce B. "Genius Denied and Reclaimed: A 40-Year Retrospect on Marshall G.S. Hodgson's The Venture of Islam – By Bruce B. Lawrence - The Marginalia Review of Books." *The Marginalia Review of Books*. Los Angeles Review of Books, 11 Nov. 2014. Web. 02 Dec. 2016.

[ii] "Latest Annual Data." United States Bureau of Labor Statistics, *Women's Bureau (WB)*. N.p., 2014. Web. 06 May 2016.

[iii] "Women in the Corporate World: Beyond the Glass Ceiling."4 May 2016, Jumeirah Messila Hotel, Kuwait.

[iv] "Women in the Corporate World: Beyond the Glass Ceiling."4 May 2016, Jumeirah Messila Hotel, Kuwait.

[v] (Interview, Female Kuwaiti Engineer)

[vi] Gordon, Michael R. "Civilians to Take U.S. Lead as Military Leaves Iraq." *The New York Times*. The New York Times, 18 Aug. 2010. Web. 11 Feb. 2017.

[vii] Crawford, Jamie. "Left behind in Iraq: Thousands of Contractors." *CNN*. Cable News Network, n.d. Web. 11 Feb. 2017.

[viii] Interview, former senior U.S. Embassy officer

[ix] Number of countries represented in Kuwait provided by Kuwait's International Diplomatic Club in 2015.

[x] "Cinescape Rules." *Kuwait Up to Date*. N.p., 16 Apr. 2016. Web and Instagram.

[xi] Stelter, Brian. "CBS Reporter Recounts a 'Merciless' Assault." *The New York Times*. The New York Times, 28 Apr. 2011. Web. 11 Feb. 2017.

[xii] Interview, State Department Officer, U.S. Embassy Kuwait, April 17, 2016

[xiii] Interview, Wife of German Ambassador, 22 April 2016

[xiv] Longva, Anh Nga. Walls Built on Sand: Migration, Exclusion, and Society in Kuwait. Boulder, CO: WestviewPress, 1997. Print. P. 114-115.

xv http://worldpopulationreview.com/countries/kuwait-population/

xvi Longva, Anh Nga. Walls Built on Sand: Migration, Exclusion, and Society in Kuwait. Boulder, CO: WestviewPress, 1997. Print. P. 122.

xvii Interview, Kuwaiti female engineer.

xviii Longva, Anh Nga. Walls Built on Sand: Migration, Exclusion, and Society in Kuwait. Boulder, CO: Westview Press, 1997. Print. P. 193.

xix Gonzalez, Alessandra L. Islamic Feminism in Kuwait: The Politics and Paradoxes. New York: Palgrave Macmillan, 2013. Print. p. 103.

xx Gonzalez, Alessandra L. Islamic Feminism in Kuwait: The Politics and Paradoxes. New York: Palgrave Macmillan, 2013. Print.

xxi "SOCIAL REFORM SOCIETY - GENERAL SECRETARIAT OF CHARITABLE WORK." Forbes Middle East, 2015. Web. 19 June 2016.

xxii Al-Mughni, Haya. "The Rise of Islamic Feminism in Kuwait." "L'émergence Du Féminisme Islamique Au Koweit." - *Open Access Library*. Revue Des Mondes Musulmans Et De La Méditerranée, Dec. 2015. Web. 18 June 2016.

xxiii Al-Mughni, Haya. "The Rise of Islamic Feminism in Kuwait." "L'émergence Du Féminisme Islamique Au Koweit." - *Open Access Library*. Revue Des Mondes Musulmans Et De La Méditerranée, Dec. 2015. Web. 18 June 2016.

xxiv Interview, Kuwaiti academic and feminist, June 2016

xxv www.ohchr.org/EN/NewsEvents/Pages/DisplayNews.aspx?NewsID=15109&#st hash.PgxIHdCr.dpuf

xxvi Al-Mughni, Haya. "The Rise of Islamic Feminism in Kuwait." "L'émergence Du Féminisme Islamique Au Koweit." - *Open Access Library*. Revue Des Mondes Musulmans Et De La Méditerranée, Dec. 2015. Web. 18 June 2016.

xxvii Interview, female Kuwaiti international relations expert.

xxviii Interview, female Kuwaiti international relations expert.

xxix Interview, female Kuwaiti international relations expert.

xxx "Profiles of Women in STE in Kuwait." *AAAS*. N.p., 20 June 2013. Web. 23 June 2016.

xxxi Gonzalez, Alessandra L. Islamic Feminism in Kuwait: The Politics and Paradoxes. New York: Palgrave Macmillan, 2013. Print. P. 74.

xxxii Mughni, Haya. *Women in Kuwait: The Politics of Gender*. London: Saqi, 1993. Print. P. 55.

xxxiii Mughni, Haya.

xxxiv Frazer, John E., and David F. Cupp. "Kuwait, Aladdin's Lamp of the Middle East." *National Geographic* 135.No. 5 (May 1969): 11. pg. Web.

xxxv Blog by local western woman who has lived in Kuwait for decades called Desert Girl.

xxxvi Interview, British expat employed in upscale western supermarket chain.

xxxvii Gonzalez, Alessandra L. Islamic Feminism in Kuwait: The Politics and Paradoxes. New York: Palgrave Macmillan, 2013. Print. P. 61.

xxxviii Ghabra, Shafeeq. "Kuwait and the Dynamics of Socio-Economic Change." *Contemporary Persian Gulf*, Barry Rubin (ed), Routledge, 2013. N. pg. Print.

xxxix Ghabra, Shafeeq.

xl Ghabra, Shafeeq.

xli Ghabra, Shafeeq.

xlii Ghabra, Shafeeq

xliii Husain, Mir Zohair. Global Islamic Politics. New York: HarperCollins College, 1995. Print. P. 46.

xliv Interview, Kuwaiti businessman, May 2016.

xlv Coulson, Noel J. *A History of Islamic Law.* Edinburgh: U, 1964. Print.P. 91.

xlvi Coulson, Noel J. *A History of Islamic Law.* Edinburgh: U, 1964. Print. P. 71.

xlvii Gonzalez, Alessandra L. Islamic Feminism in Kuwait: The Politics and Paradoxes. New York: Palgrave Macmillan, 2013. Print. P. 63.

xlviii Ghabra, Shafeeq.

xlix Kuwait Times, Feb 16, 2016, "Controversy Over KTV Comedic Dance

l Interview, Embassy Officer, U.S. Embassy, April 17, 2016

li https://abdurrahman.org/2015/06/04/a-great-piece-of-advice-to-the-men-and-women-who-listen-to-music/

lii Bourisly, Khaled H. *Shipmasters of Kuwait: A Glorious Era Before the Oil Discovery.* First ed. Kuwait City: Khaled H. Bourisly, 2008. Print. P. 122

liii Bourisly, Khaled H. P. 148

liv Ajami, Fouad. *The Arab Predicament: Arab Political Thought and Practice since 1967.* Cambridge: Cambridge UP, 1981. Print. P. 139

lv Interview, senior official at the United Nations office in Kuwait.

lvi Husain, Mir Zohair. Global Islamic Politics. New York: HarperCollins College, 1995. Print. P. 48.

lvii Interview, Kuwaiti woman.

lviii Al-Nakib, Mai. "Unity Without Islamism in Kuwait: It is Time to Blaze Forth Once Again." Arab Times, 1 July 2015.

lix "Land Reform in Egypt." *Wikipedia.* Wikimedia Foundation, n.d. Web. 02 May 2016.

lx Ajami, Fouad. *The Arab Predicament: Arab Political Thought and Practice since 1967.* Cambridge: Cambridge UP, 1981. Print. P. 126.

lxi Interview, Kuwait University Communications Professor, 2015

lxii Internet.

lxiii Ibn Khaldoun, 'Abd Al-Rahman Ibn Mohammad. Translated from the Arabic by Franz Rosenthal. Abridged and Edited by N. J. Dawood. *The Muqaddimah: An Introduction to History.* London: Routledge and Kegan Paul, 1967. Print. P. 98.

lxiv Nydell, Margaret K. Understanding Arabs: A Guide for Modern times. Boston ; London: Intercultural, 2006. Print, P. 75.

lxv Jalili, Ismail K. "Consanguinity - Cousin Marriages and Childhood Blindness." *Consanguinity - Cousin Marriages and Childhood Blindness.* N.p., 2015. Web. 13 Jan. 2016.

lxvi "500 Kuwaitis Suffer from Thalasemia." Kuwait News Agency. N.p., 29 Nov. 2008. Web.

lxvii Interview, local five-star hotel manager.

lxviii Al-Fuzai, Muna. "Shocking Divorce Rate in Kuwait." *Kuwait Times.* N.p., 17 Sept. 2015. Web. 24 Feb. 2017.

lxix Interview, Jesuit Catholic Priest in Ankara, Turkey, 2010, who belonged to the Missionaries of Africa, commonly known as the White Fathers or the Society of the Missionaries of Africa.

lxx Nydell, Margaret K. *Understanding Arabs: A Guide for Modern times.* Boston ; London: Intercultural, 2006. Print, P. 86.

lxxi Desert Girl Blog. "DG Ramadan Advice." DG Ramadan Advice. N.p., 13 Aug. 2009, Web. 25 Feb. 2017.

[lxxii] "Living in Kuwait." *Basic Laws and Regulations in Kuwait.* N.p., n.d. Web. 15 Jan. 2016.

[lxxiii] Kuwait Times, D&G Unveils Designs for Muslim Women, 10 January 2016.

[lxxiv] Kuwait Times, D&G Unveils Designs for Muslim Women, 10 January 2016.

[lxxv] "Embassy of the State of Kuwait." *Embassy of the State of Kuwait.* N.p., n.d. Web. 21 Jan. 2016.)

[lxxvi] "Kuwait Constitution." Kuwait Constitution. N.p., n.d. Web. 25 Feb. 2017.

[lxxvii] Qattan, Lidia Al. *Rulers of Kuwait.* Kuwait City: L. Al Qattan, 2004. Print.

[lxxviii] Interview, founders of Abolish 153 Campaign.

[lxxix] The Diffusion of Law: The Movement of Laws and Norms Around the World, p.33.

[lxxx] Lovell, Mary S. Rebel Heart: The Scandalous Life of Jane Digby. New York: W.W. Norton, 1995. Print.

[lxxxi] Kristof, Nicholas D., and Sheryl WuDunn. Half the Sky: Turning Oppression into Opportunity for Women Worldwide. New York: Alfred A. Knopf, 2009. Print. p.82.

[lxxxii] Kristof, p. 82

[lxxxiii] Lipka, Michael. "Muslims and Islam: Key Findings in the U.S. and around the World." *Pew Research Center RSS.* Pew Research Center, 07 Dec. 2015. Web. 16 Dec. 2015, p. 89.

[lxxxiv] Lipka, p. 89.

[lxxxv] Daily Mail, Chris Pleasance, Oct. 10, 2014.

[lxxxvi] Kristof, Nicholas D., and Sheryl WuDunn. Half the Sky: Turning Oppression into Opportunity for Women Worldwide. New York: Alfred A. Knopf, 2009. Print. p.82.

[lxxxvii] Kristof, Nicholas D., and Sheryl WuDunn. p.81.

[lxxxviii] Coulson, Noel J. A History of Islamic Law. Edinburgh: U, 1964. Print. P. 14.

[lxxxix] N.J. Coulson, A History of Islamic Law, p.14

[xc] N.J. Coulson, A History of Islamic Law, p.14

[xci] Gonzalez, Alessandra L. Islamic Feminism in Kuwait: The Politics and Paradoxes. New York: Palgrave Macmillan, 2013. Print. p.35.

[xcii] Gonzalez, Alessandra L.

[xciii] Presentation by Zannuba Rahman Wahid, February 1, 2016.

[xciv] Gonzalez, Alessandra L. Islamic Feminism in Kuwait: The Politics and Paradoxes. New York: Palgrave Macmillan, 2013. Print, p. 35.

[xcv] Abolish 153 Campaign website.

[xcvi] Interview, Abolish 153 board members.

[xcvii] Cohn, Laura. "15 Female Candidates Ran for Parliament in Kuwait's Latest Election. Only This Woman Won." Women in Kuwait: 15 Female Candidates Ran for Office. Only 1 Won. | Fortune.com. Fortune, 28 Nov. 2016. Web. 08 Jan. 2017.

[xcviii] "Kuwaiti Women Win Passport Rights." - Al Jazeera English. N.p., 21 Oct. 2009. Web. 28 Jan. 2016.

[xcix] "Kuwaiti Women Win Passport Rights." - Al Jazeera English. N.p., 21 Oct. 2009. Web. 28 Jan. 2016.

[c] The Status of National Women Married to Non-Nationals in the Gulf Cooperation Council Countries, p25.

[ci] Interview, American woman married to a Kuwaiti citizen.

[cii] Roy, Chaitali. "Insight: A Conversation with Dr Massouma Al-Mubarak." *Arab Times* [Kuwait City] 11 May 2015: 12. Print.

[ciii] Vargas, Elizabeth. "Person of the Week: Dr. Massouma Al-Mubarak." *ABCNEWS*. ABC News World News Tonight, 2005. Web. 29 Jan. 2016.

[civ] Interview with Alshaya executives.

[cv] Al-Qabas newspaper, 7 February 2016.

[cvi] Bourisly, Khaled H. *Shipmasters of Kuwait: A Glorious Era Before the Oil Discovery*. First ed. Kuwait City: Khaled H. Bourisly, 2008. Print. p. 15 - 16.

[cvii] Mughni, Haya. *Women in Kuwait: The Politics of Gender*. London: Saqi, 1993. Print. p. 22.

[cviii] Mansfield, Peter. *The New Arabians*. Chicago: J.G. Ferguson Pub., 1981. Print. p. 106.

[cix] Mughni, Haya. *Women in Kuwait: The Politics of Gender*. London: Saqi, 1993. Print. p. 23.

[cx] Mughni, Haya. p. 24.

[cxi] Kuwait National Museum.

[cxii] Bourisly, Khaled H. *Shipmasters of Kuwait: A Glorious Era Before the Oil Discovery*. First ed. Kuwait City: Khaled H. Bourisly, 2008. Print. p. 189.

[cxiii] Mansfield, Peter. *The New Arabians*. Chicago: J.G. Ferguson Pub., 1981. Print. p. 109.

[cxiv] Interview, Kuwait Oil Company employees.

[cxv] Qattan, Lidia Al. *Rulers of Kuwait*. Kuwait City: L. Al Qattan, 2004. Print, p. 243.

cxvi Mansfield, Peter. *The New Arabians*. Chicago: J.G. Ferguson Pub., 1981. Print. p. 110.

cxvii "Our Story." *Kuwait Petroleum Company*. N.p., n.d. Web. 11 Feb. 2017.

cxviii "World Fact Book - Kuwait." *World Fact Book - Kuwait*. Central Intelligence Agency, 2015. Web. 21 July 2015.

cxix Kemp, Geoffrey, and Robert E. Harkavy. *Strategic Geography and the Changing Middle East*. Washington, DC: Carnegie Endowment for International Peace, 1997. Print. p. 125.

cxx Bentley, Elliot PaJovi, Pat Minczeski, and Jovi Juan. "Which Oil Producers Are Breaking Even?" *WSJ*. Wall Street Journal, 27 Nov. 2014. Web. 04 Aug. 2015.

cxxi Bentley, Elliot PaJovi, Pat Minczeski, and Jovi Juan. "Which Oil Producers Are Breaking Even?" *WSJ*. Wall Street Journal, 27 Nov. 2014. Web. 04 Aug. 2015.

cxxii *Kuwait Investment Authority*. N.p., 2015. Web. 25 Apr. 2016.

cxxiii Jaber, Ahmad. "58 Percent Unemployed Kuwaitis Unwilling to Work in Private Sector – Efforts to Kuwaitize Private Sector Largely Failed." *Kuwait Times*. N.p., 18 Apr. 2016. Web. 25 Apr. 2016.

cxxiv Atwood, Ed. "Kuwait Confirms New Pay Deals as Strikes Continue." *Arabian Business*. N.p., 19 Mar. 2012. Web. 11 Feb. 2017.

cxxv Longva, Anh Nga. Walls Built on Sand: Migration, Exclusion, and Society in Kuwait. Boulder, CO: WestviewPress, 1997. Print. P. 65 and P. 72.

cxxvi Interview, American environmentalist and substitute science teacher at local private high school.

cxxvii Interview, American environmentalist and substitute science teacher at local private high school.

cxxviii Khadada M, The cost of asthma in Kuwait.

[cxxix] Gulf Insider: WHO 09/22/2014.

[cxxx] Kuwait Times, 04/11/2013, Environmental disasters; Interview, U.S. Embassy Officer.

[cxxxi] Interview, Bahraini Naval Pilot to Ambassador, 15 Feb 2016; Kuwait: The Effects of Oil Drilling.

[cxxxii] Interview, Jassim Mostafa Boodai, Integrated Holding Co. April 2016

[cxxxiii] KT, Kuwait Ranks No. 4, 29 May 2014; Interiew with Dr. Azizi, 3 Febrary 2016

[cxxxiv] Correspondent, Winter 2015; Arab Times, 31 Jan 2016, Pediatric Obesity

[cxxxv] Interview, Dr. Bahareh Azizi, February 3, 2016.

[cxxxvi] "Health in Islam (part 1 of 4): A Holistic Approach." - *The Religion of Islam*. The Cooperative Office of Dawah in Rawdah, 17 Nov. 2008. Web. 18 June 2016.

[cxxxvii] Interview, American woman married to a Kuwaiti who raised her children in Kuwait.

[cxxxviii] Interview, same American woman.

[cxxxix] Interview, same American woman.

[cxl] Qattan, Lidia Al. *Rulers of Kuwait*. Kuwait City: L. Al Qattan, 2004. Print.

[cxli] LUCKY. "Kuwait Airways' New 777-300s Might Actually Be Competitive - One Mile at a Time."One Mile at a Time. Boarding Area, 14 Nov. 2016. Web. 16 Dec. 2016.

[cxlii] "The World Factbook: KUWAIT." *Central Intelligence Agency*. Central Intelligence Agency, 12 Jan. 2017. Web. 19 Feb. 2017.

[cxliii] http://news.kuwaittimes.net/website/kuwaiti-woman-killed-by-maid/

[cxliv] Longva, Anh Nga. Walls Built on Sand: Migration, Exclusion, and Society in Kuwait. Boulder, CO: WestviewPress, 1997. Print.

[cxlv] Interview, Filippina tailor in Kuwait.

cxlvi Longva, Anh Nga. Walls Built on Sand: Migration, Exclusion, and Society in Kuwait. Boulder, CO: WestviewPress, 1997. Print. P. 54.

cxlvii Interview, Dr. Hilal Al-Sayer, Kuwait Red Crescent Society.

cxlviii Interview, Dr. Hilal Al-Sayer, March 2016.

cxlix "Kuwait - Dr Hilal Al-Sayer, Deputy President of the Kuwait Red Crescent Society." The Worldfolio, 2014. Web. 14 May 2016.

cl Centre, UNESCO World Heritage. "Ancient City of Damascus." UNESCO World Heritage Centre. N.p., n.d. Web. 19 Feb. 2017.

cli Lovel, Mary S. "Rebel Heart: The Scandalous Life Jane Digby. New York: W.W. Norton, 1995. Print.

clii Lovel, Mary S. "Rebel Heart: The Scandalous Life Jane Digby. New York: W.W. Norton, 1995. Print.

cliii "GUST Students Hit New World Record with Charity Clothes Drive." Gulf University for Science and Technology. N.p., 31 Jan. 2015. Web. 17 Oct. 2015.

cliv Dickinson, Elizabeth. "Playing with Fire: Why Private Gulf Financing for Syria's Extremist Rebels Risks Igniting Sectarian Conflict at Home." "The Saban Center for Middle East Policy at Brookings 16 (2013): n. page. Brookings Institute, Dec. 2013. Web. 05 Aug. 2015.

clv Dickinson, Elizabeth. "Playing with Fire: Why Private Gulf Financing for Syria's Extremist Rebels Risks Igniting Sectarian Conflict at Home." "The Saban Center for Middle East Policy at Brookings 16 (2013): n. page. Brookings Institute, Dec. 2013. Web. 05 Aug. 2015.

clvi Howell, W. Nathaniel. Strangers When We Met: A Century of American Community in Kuwait. Washington, DC: New Academia, 2016. Print, P. 393.

clvii Hagagy, Ahmed. "Islamic State Suicide Bomber Kills 27, Wounds 227 in Kuwait Mosque." Reuters.

clviii Mandhai, Shafik. "Bidoon Fleeing Kuwait, Stuck in the Calais 'jungle'" - *Al Jazeera English*. N.p., 29 Mar. 2016. Web. 02 May 2016.

clix Spencer, Richard. "Kuwait Attack: Islamic State Suicide Bombing at Shia Mosque Kills 27."*The Telegraph.* Telegraph Media Group, 26 June 2015. Web. 19 Feb. 2017.

clx Husain, Mir Zohair. Global Islamic Politics. New York: HarperCollins College, 1995. Print. P. 9.

clxi Fernea, Elizabeth Warnock. *Guest of the Sheik an Ethnography of an Iraqi Village.* New York: Anchor, 1965. Print, p. 110 and p. 194.

clxii Husain, Mir Zohair. Global Islamic Politics. New York: HarperCollins College, 1995. Print. p. 9.

clxiii Hagagy, Ahmed. "Islamic State Suicide Bomber Kills 27, Wounds 227 in Kuwait Mosque."*Reuters.* Thomson Reuters, 26 June 2015. Web. 19 Feb. 2017.

clxiv Harby, Mahmoud, and Ahmed Hagagy. "Kuwait Seizes Arms, Holds Suspects in Militant Plot: Local Media." *Reuters.* Thomson Reuters, 13 Aug. 2015. Web. 19 Feb. 2017.

clxv "Unity without Islamism in Kuwait: It is Time to Blaze Forth Once Again," Al-Nakib, Mai. Arab Times, 1 July 2015.

clxvi "Unity without Islamism in Kuwait: It is Time to Blaze Forth Once Again," Al-Nakib, Mai. Arab Times, 1 July 2015.

clxvii Freer, Courtney. "The Rise of Pragmatic Islamism in Kuwait's PostArab Spring Opposition Movement." Project on Working Relations with the Islamic World" *Brookings Institute.* N.p., Aug. 2015. Web. 19 Feb. 2017.

clxviii Al-Nakib, Rania. "Education and Democratic Development in Kuwait: Citizens in Waiting."*Chatham House.* N.p., Mar. 2015. Web. 19 Feb. 2017.

clxix Al-Nakib, Mai. "Unity without Islamism in Kuwait." *Arabtimes.com.* Arab TImes, 01 July 2015. Web. 27 July 2015.

clxx Al-Nakib, Rania. "Education and Democratic Development in Kuwait: Citizens in Waiting." *Chatham House*. N.p., 8 Apr. 2015. Web. 20 May 2016.

clxxi Al-Nakib, Rania. "Education and Democratic Development in Kuwait: Citizens in Waiting." *Chatham House*. N.p., 8 Apr. 2015. Web. 20 May 2016.

clxxii "Back to School in Mosul: The ISIS Curriculum.: The Daily Beast. The Daily Beast Company, 29 Oct 2015. Web 10 Feb. 2017.

clxxiii Saul, Stephanie. "The Mideast Came to Idaho State. It Wasn't the Best Fit." *The New York Times*. The New York Times, 21 Mar. 2016. Web. 08 Dec. 2016.

clxxiv Interview, NUKS-USA president.

clxxv Interview, Rebecca Ness, Superintendent of American School of Kuwait.

clxxvi Interview, U.S. Embassy Public Affairs Officer.

clxxvii Conference on "Women in the Corporate World: Beyond the Glass Ceiling."4 May 2016, Jumeirah Messila Beach Hotel, Kuwait.

clxxviii Abualarub, Samer Yousef. "The Problems with Kuwait's Struggling Educational System." *Friday Times.* , 10 June 2016. N.p., n.d. Web.

clxxix Interview, American teacher in Kuwaiti private school.

clxxx Abualarub, Samer Yousef. "The Problems with Kuwait's Struggling Educational System." *Friday Times.* , 10 June 2016. N.p., n.d. Web.

clxxxi Interview, American teacher in Kuwaiti private school.

clxxxii Interview, American elementary school teacher in private Kuwaiti school.

clxxxiii Interview, American elementary school teacher in private Kuwaiti school.

clxxxiv Interview, professor at Kuwait University.

[clxxxv] *"Kuwait Times"*. 19 May 2016. "Education Budget Increases to KD 1.7 Billion, Quality Retreats - Corruption Rampant in MoE: Essa - Kuwait Times.

[clxxxvi] Abualarub, Samer Yousef. "The Problems with Kuwait's Struggling Educational System." *Friday Times.*, 10 June 2016. N.p., n.d. Web.

[clxxxvii] GCC education ministers adopt Kuwait work paper in Riyadh meeting, KUNA, 21 April 2016

[clxxxviii] GCC education ministers adopt Kuwait work paper in Riyadh meeting, KUNA, 21 April 2016

[clxxxix] "Kuwait National Curriculum and Standards." *www.moe.edu.kw*. Kuwait Ministry of Education, 2014. Web. 26 Jan. 2017, p. 104.

[cxc] "Kuwait National Curriculum and Standards." *www.moe.edu.kw*. Kuwait Ministry of Education, 2014. Web. 26 Jan. 2017, p. 104.

[cxci] Rajab, Jehan S. *Invasion Kuwait: An Englishwoman's Tale.* London: Radcliffe, 1993. Print.

[cxcii] Copies of the textbooks provided to U.S. Embassy Kuwait.

[cxciii] "Kuwait Energy." *Kuwait Energy*. N.p., 16 July 2012. Web. 19 Feb. 2017.

[cxciv] Interview, Sara Akbar, January 2016.

[cxcv] Interview, U.S. Embassy Officer, September 2016

[cxcvi]www.army.mil/article/157534/School_program_commemorates_Kuwaiti_Liberation__Operation_Desert_Storm

[cxcvii] Interview, senior U.S. Embassy officer.

[cxcviii]www.army.mil/article/157534/School_program_commemorates_Kuwaiti_Liberation__Operation_Desert_Storm